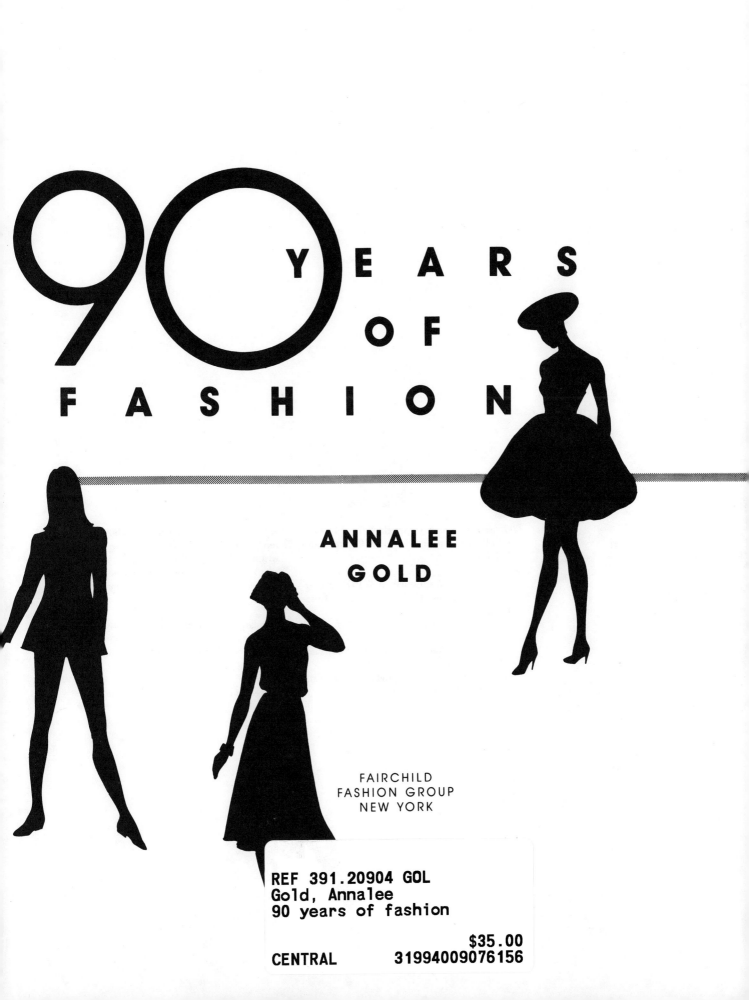

90 YEARS OF FASHION

ANNALEE
GOLD

FAIRCHILD
FASHION GROUP
NEW YORK

Book and Cover Design by Jaye Zimet

90 Years of Fashion, Copyright © 1991 by Fairchild Fashion Group, Division of Capital Cities Media, Inc.

75 Years of Fashion, Copyright © 1975 by Fairchild Publications, Division of Capital Cities Media, Inc.
Third Printing, 1987
Second Printing, 1979
60 Years of Fashion, Copyright © 1963, Fairchild Publications, Inc.
50 Years of Fashion, Copyright © 1950 Fairchild Publications, Inc.

Standard Book Number: 87005-680-8

Library of Congress Catalog Card Number: 90-81848

Printed in the United States of America

ACKNOWLEDGMENTS

We wish to thank Olga Kontzias, our editor, and Bina Abling, our fashion illustrator. We are also indebted to the late Richard Thornton, who contributed art to the earlier edition, and to those staff editors and artists of *Women's Wear Daily*, some anonymous, who created and contributed to the first two books in this series. We owe a very special debt to Merle Thomason, costume librarian of Fairchild Publications. Each time we said, "I don't suppose you have. . . ," she dived into her files and emerged triumphantly with just what we needed.

C O N T E N T S

I N T R O D U C T I O N

Ninety Years of Fashion is the latest in a series that started out as "Fifty Years" and went on, first, to "Sixty Years" and then, to "Seventy-Five." Our book now spans nine decades—almost a century!

All categories are updated, so that our history remains an accurate, down-to-earth guide to the clothes women wore from 1900 on. We have focused on the highlights of each era, so that our readers can follow the path of fashion change.

Details like the shape of shoes, the outline of hair and the length of skirts will help our readers compare the 1960s to the 1920s, or the 1920s to the 1980s. The expanded silhouette section provides an overview of evolving shapes.

The format of the previous three editions remains; text and illustrations appear close to each other, for reading ease.

We hope the new edition will be useful to students, teachers, retailers, designers, manufacturers and to everyone in the fashion industry. And we hope to appeal to a more general group of readers—those who are interested in fashion for its own sake.

MERGING OF THE MARKETS

There was a time when there were sharp dividing lines between one clothing market and another—dresses, coats and suits, sportswear and separates and others. As time passed those dividing lines blurred. Suits looked like two-piece dresses. Coats were sold with dresses in either the coat or the dress department. Women wore beach dresses at home. By 1990, most clothing was classified simply as formal or informal.

SIMPLIFICATION OF FASHION

The sportswear influence grew from the 1940s on. By 1990, T-shirts, sweaters, skirts, pants and other separates were what many women wanted to wear most of the time. Separates could be dressy, too, but the casual, low-key sportswear approach became more and more popular during the 1970s and 1980s. Elaborate styles, trims and construction details began to disappear. This simplification had to do with the way women lived, but it also had an economic cause.

Costs were increasing steadily. Fabrics, production, labor—every element that went into a garment went in with extra dollars. Manufacturers tried to keep a ceiling on costs by choosing less expensive fabrics, eliminating construction details and trims and shifting production from the United States to overseas countries, especially in Asia, where labor costs were lower. Even

so, the price of clothing rose sharply through the 1980s. By the end of the decade, only a small group of manufacturers were able to offer elaborate styles in sumptuous fabrics—and only a small group of women could afford to buy them.

CHANGES IN FASHION ATTITUDES

From the 1960s on, sources of fashion direction multiplied. Paris was important, but so were Rome, Milan, Tokyo and the latest youth look from the street. There was much less desire to emulate, imitate and follow. More women charted their own fashion course, following their inclinations and their pocketbooks. As clothing prices rose, some turned to the new, sophisticated mailorder catalogues. Shopping by mail was no longer only for the farmer's wife.

Recognition of more than one standard of beauty had begun in the 1960s. By the 1980s, fashion magazines used a variety of black and Oriental models. Non-white women no longer felt obliged to dye or bleach hair and skin in a sad effort to imitate Western European ideals.

As the political climate began to change early in 1990, there were predictions that Eastern Europe and Asia would develop their own fashion centers and set new standards.

In another ten years, the phrase, "turn of the century" will take on a new meaning. Who knows what changes the new century will bring? Whatever they are, they will reflect social, political and economic conditions, as fashion always does.

While we cannot predict the future, we hope that this book will help our readers understand what has happened so far, and perhaps, lead them to make some predictions of their own.

1

DRESSES

1900

In **1900**, Paris was the center of fashion for the entire world, with Worth, Lanvin and Callot Soeurs heading the great couture. This was the age of elegance, of fabulous luxury, of great skills and low wages, of beautiful workmanship and of rich, interesting fabrics. The costumes were characterized by exquisite detail and feminine softness. French models were slavishly copied in each minute detail by dressmakers throughout the world. Customers demanded exact reproductions.

The costume chosen for this period is of chiffon and lace but there were many similar models, some without trains, made of the finest batistes and voiles trimmed with Irish crochet and Valenciennes lace.

By **1913** there was a complete change in silhouette. The skirt became straight—in

1913

1919

many cases smaller at the hemline. Some were draped and crossed in the front. Clothes had a more sophisticated look.

In **1919**, the French dressmakers tried to introduce a shorter shirt, but the more conservative Americans clung to the lower line. This dress, worn at Palm Beach with a little summer fur, has a formality difficult to associate with sand and salt air.

Paul Poiret took the corsets off the more style-concious women of Paris before the war, but the unlined dress of softer contour was not adopted generally until the early twenties. It was through Poiret that the industrial art of Paris found again a faint touch of the East and Near East. In this dress of **1923**, he used the oriental cut in the sleeve. The ornament is Near Eastern in character.

Lanvin's "robe de style" was ageless. Although it was early in the twenties—we show a **1923** version—when Lanvin introduced "le robe," she was still making it when the Germans invaded Paris in 1940. A serious student of design, she strove for genuine beauty in her work—never style tricks—and her costumes were usually designed from documents having a long style life.

By **1926** the skirt was short. For evening, the beaded sheath, originally introduced by Callot, had won its popularity.

Gabrielle Chanel, who had the reputation of being the first modern dressmaker, will always be remembered for two of her great contributions to the fashion world: her simple jersey two-piece dress (she was the first to use jersey) and her untrimmed, soft,

1926

1923

1923

11

1927

1927

1927

flowing chiffon evening dress. They won the hearts of women young and old and brought a new era to dress designing. We show a jersey costume and a chiffon evening dress, both dated **1927**.

In **1927** the house of Premet had great success with the introduction of the "Garconne" dress said to have been inspired by Franklin Simon's Bramley dress worn by American tourists traveling in Paris.

For some time the French couture had been trying in various ways to lengthen the skirt line, but it was not until 1928, or perhaps one should say **1929**, that Louise Boulanger successfully introduced her chiffon evening dresses, short in front and trailing in the back. At last she had found a style women would accept, and the longer skirt soon followed.

Madeleine Vionnet, the greatest creative artist of them all, was the first to introduce a dress depending entirely on cut for its appeal. Her famous bias cut enabled her to make dresses that slipped on over the head (needing no fastenings) and were devoid of all trimmings. This revolutionary idea was first shown in 1919, but she continued to use the principle throughout her entire career as a dressmaker.

One of the dresses we have chosen is from **1932**; softly draped, with the designer's characteristic cowl neckline. Another, dated **1935**, is side-draped and also features a subtly bared back. (Many gowns of the thirties bared the back, often to a point below the waist.)

Mainbocher's lingerie dress, **1935**, is a two-piece navy wool, with the lacy white collar and cuffs so typical of the thirties.

1932

1935

1929

1935

13

1938

1938

1943

1944

14

Crepe dress with gathering and leg-o'-mutton sleeves, **1938**, carries out the fitted silhouette with wider shoulders. Elsa Schiaparelli's two-piece outfit, **1938**, combines her famous bolero jacket with a print crepe dress. (The print was white, rose and fuchsia on black grounds.) Skirts were moving up towards the knee. The waistline was more definitely marked. Styling became simplified after World War II began.

The war brought many restrictions to the fashion industries, among them L-85, the law restricting yardage in clothing. The shirtwaist dress grew in popularity during this time, 1941–1945, and became a basic working girl's dress along with the factory worker's overalls. We show a shirtwaist coat dress, **1943**, and a two-tone style, **1944**.

Christian Dior probably more than anyone else, started us on a new type of costume when these restrictions were lifted after the war. His famous first collection in **1947** introduced the "New Look," feminine curves, tiny waist and great fullness in longer skirts.

In America the name of Claire McCardell stood for American design uninfluenced by Paris. Her monastic dress, **1949**, in jersey with criss-cross string belt at midriff had a lasting influence.

By **1950**, lines of skirts had slimmed, and the casual shirtdress with push-up sleeves was worn in satins as well as wools for all occasions.

1950

1947

1949

15

1954

1955

1958

16

1958

1959

1959

The shutting off of fashion imports from France during the war period, 1939–1945, gave impetus to American designers who began to receive credit on a par with foreign couturiers.

New silhouettes appeared rapidly in the decade from 1950 to 1960. The biggest influence in this decade was that of Cristobal Balenciaga who, after the war was acknowledged as the greatest designer of all. About 1954 he broke away from extremely fitted lines to a new "semi-fit," close to the body in front but easy and straight in back, collars away from the neck, soft round shoulders and shorter sleeves. This new concept influenced every category of fashion.

The high Empire-line bolero and sheath dress of **1954** is typical of this new rounded unfitted ease at the top of the body.

Anne Fogarty's name stands out (in early **1955**) for creating a "Paper Doll" look which swept the country. She introduced the bouffant crinoline petticoat under shorter full skirts, with wide, cinched belts and prim little shirt tops.

The year 1957 marked a major revolution in fashion, with the introduction of the "chemise" or "sack" dress by Balenciaga and Givenchy simultaneous with its appearance in Italian collections. This completely loose unbelted dress caught on in **1958** but was so hastily copied and badly made that the style became ridiculous and died quickly, to be revived in 1960.

The same year, **1958**, Dior created a successful "Trapeze" dress, also unbelted but widening into a flare from a fitted bosom, somewhat like a child's dress.

The simple straight dress with its own jacket, called the "costume," was the biggest dress news in **1959**. Printed silks were of superior design; black and white were considered chic. The dress, **1959**, with kimono top and wide obi sash reflected the Far Eastern influences permeating Paris and U.S. design.

1962

1960

The rise of the sportswear market which influenced all fashions from coats to formal evening wear brings us in **1960** to an all-time favorite, the two-piece dress. A loose, sleeveless, high-necked overblouse and slim skirt in brilliant solid colors became the uniform for all seasons. This stark design was forecast by Balenciaga and Hubert Givenchy in Paris and was adapted by the majority of other designers everywhere.

The most glowing exponent of this pared-down way of dressing was the wife of the late President, Mrs. John F. Kennedy (Jacqueline Kennedy Onassis).

A few belted dresses were popular during

1963

1963

the early 1960s, despite the loosening of the silhouette. Norman Norell designed this elegant versioin of "the little black dress" in **1962**. The wide leather belt that marks the waist is a fashion on its way out.

The incoming chemise silhouette was interpreted in many ways, for instance, in a lace shirtdress, **1963**. (The shirtdress is a constantly recurring theme.) A fisherman's smock by Yves Saint Laurent, **1963**, is another version of the chemise.

In the same year: Dior's evening chemise in bright pink with beads has a low back and flounce that vary the silhouette. Short evening gowns were now very much in fashion and were no longer known as "cocktail dresses," a term that expired with the fifties.

One of the most popular dresses of **1965** was the Saint Laurent chemise in bright blocks of color inspired by the Dutch painter Mondrian.

Skirt hemlines continued to rise. Miniskirts were followed by even briefer micro-minis, some barely covering the thigh. One exception to the brief skirt was this two-piece dress inspired by the film, *Dr. Zhivago*. (It was the exception that proved the rule. The rule was short skirts.) Our **1967** two-piece dress combines white crepe Russian blouse with navy skirt and boots.

1963

1965

1967

1968

1970

1968

A little girl looked developed as skirt hemlines rose. The ruffled front chemise, **1968**, is made of sheer silk. Covered-up clothes revealed the body beneath using cut-outs and see-through inserts of sheer fabric, as in a **1968** evening gown of white crepe with see-through midriff, accented by bands of jeweling.

The Dr. Zhivago look never caught on in a big way, but it did foreshadow a more important move towards longer lengths. In 1970, the European and American fashion establishment sponsored the midi, or mid-calf skirt, also known as the *longuette*. Again, American women rejected the length; the change was too sudden and too drastic. Unsure and confused about hemlines, they turned to pants for street wear.

There were also pants for evening wear. The **1970** two-piece evening outfit by James Galanos represents the highest level of fashion. Galanos is known for his cut and shaping. Here, a blouson top combines with full pajamas of circular cut.

What is a dress? What are separates? What is sportswear? These questions were more difficult to answer from 1970 on. In fact, many dresses were sportswear. The **1972** T-shirt dress of polyester jersey was a good example. Young designers like Clovis Ruffin were associated with these dresses. At a much higher price level there was Halston, a designer first known for millinery. His updated classic designs seemed to catch the spirit of the times. We show two of his **1972** styles. First, the caftan, accompanied by Elsa Peretti's ivory egg pendant, typical of the new "real" jewelry stressing natural, relatively inexpensive materials as opposed to diamonds and other precious stones. Second, Halston's shirt-coatdress that appeared as hemlines began to come down. Young girls were still wearing micro-minis, especially in the summer.

The **1973** dress with raglan sleeves and stitching detail shows a loosening and softening of the silhouette, with its deeper armholes and eased waistline.

1972

1972

1972

1973

21

1974

1978

1976

1987

The **1974** wool jersey dress in two prints is another expression of the softer silhouette. In **1976**, Yves Saint Laurent launched his "rich peasant" look, shown here. Long, full skirts, mixed prints, drawstring blouses and gathering softened the silhouette. Vests, jackets, scarves and shawls were worn in layers.

In **1978**, Scott Barrie showed his satin "slip dress" for evening wear, and slit the hemline deeply for a touch of drama. At this time, hemlines were wandering from knee to mid-calf; there were no drastic changes. Women found that boots went well with longer skirts; western leather boots were an important footwear fashion.

By the 1980s, skirt lengths began to rise and padded shoulders were fashionable—the look was far stiffer and broader than it had been in the 1940s. There was a revival of the mini; when Christian Lacroix designed his "pouf" dresses for Patou, he became an overnight sensation. But the pouf was impractical and hard to wear. We show a **1987** version; the pouf had a short life, but it made history at a time when there was little fashion news. Emanuel Ungaro did a series of short, draped dresses; we show one from **1988**. Short, tight skirts had a strong following among the young. But working women could not wear them; the blatant sexual message was inappropriate.

Mary Ann Restivo updated the coat dress in **1988**, cutting it to a just-above-the knee length. Evening gowns also hit above the knees, as in this one-shoulder draped chiffon, by Bill Blass, **1989**.

Geoffrey Beene's full-length silk evening gown, **1989**, with its artfully cut-out back, veiled with sheer fabric, showed that there are many ways of revealing the body.

As the 1990s began, designers showed extremely short skirts for both day and evening. Everyone continued to talk about skirt lengths, saying, among other things, how unimportant they were.

1989

1989

1988

1988

23

2

COATS

1900

The cloth coat of the early part of the 20th century was a most important part of a woman's wardrobe, because dresses were worn more often than suits. This led to the introduction of ensembles about **1910**. We find many elaborate dresses with coats to match for all seasons of the year.

Some were dressy combinations of velvet and chiffon. Many more were tailored of broadcloth and other woolen fabrics. Even in summer, silk or linen elaborately trimmed with braid or embroidery was used.

About this time the first fur-lined coats were introduced, usually with linings of squirrel—the gray and white pelts suppos-

1915

1910

edly coming from the bellies of the animals. These coats had large collars of lynx, gray squirrel or other types of fur.

By **1915** the silhouette had changed and the band of fur was used around the bottom of the coat to accent the hemline.

By **1919** the interest had again shifted and the bulk was at the top of the garment. Capes were important and we find them in all lengths from short to full length models. The dolman coat is another interpretation of this same feeling. After World War I, France, whose cotton and woolen mills were badly damaged causing a scarcity of fine cottons and woolens, turned to the silks of Lyons in the south of France where pro-duction was uninterrupted by the war. At this time silk underwear was introduced, replacing the fine batistes, nainsooks and handkerchief linens. The couture turned again to the ensemble where silk could be used for dresses.

Little straight coats of wool which could be worn over several different silk dresses came into fashion in **1927**. The suit dis-appeared almost completely and it was the great era of soft silk crepe de chine, flat crepe and satin dresses worn by women of all ages. Few people knew what caused this radical change in style. The couture care-fully concealed their reasons for stressing the ensemble.

1927

1919

1919

1934

1942

1942

1936

By **1934** the tremendous vogue for silver fox had arrived. Coat designers capitalized on this by making full-length, fitted coats with various styles in the fox collars. Many were the large, full models which framed the face and extended to the waistline.

In **1936** Schiaparelli made a coat with a collarless neckline of the dressmaker type with the accent on the sleeves, very different from the simple coats we now associate with this neckline.

World War II brought a tendency toward severity, with many masculine styles for women, among them the Chesterfield, **1942**, and the officer's coat. The feminine counterpart to these was the fitted princess coat with small fur collar and cuffs, **1942**.

1943

1945

1947

1950

The wartime demand for practical fashions developed the strictly tailored suit worn with a simple, straight, often fur-lined coat, **1943**, a fashion revived from a quarter of a century before.

The simple sport coat of **1945**, sometimes worn belted, had a long life and in later years became the "shortie" or "topper." Besides being wearable over a suit or dress it was adaptable to sportswear.

In **1947** the advent of the "New Look" introduced the "tent" coat, the long full coat which could be worn over padded hips and full skirts.

In **1950** excessive fullness was removed from coats either in actual yardage or in effect.

1955

1957

1958

1959

In **1955** coats had slimmed down to a narrower body line—with soft rounded shoulders—and closed up the front to small collars. Camel's hair fabric and color were big favorites, as was gray flannel.

The status coat at this period was the vicuna wraparound with sweeping fullness, dolman push-up sleeves and often a fur collar. Its peak of popularity was **1957**.

The loden cloth and loden green color sport coat with a raccoon collar swept the country in **1958**, starting on campus as a sport coat and ending in the city for working women. Short versions, called "car coats," were worn by women living in the suburbs, who spent much time driving; the short length was more comfortable for sliding in and out of cars.

A double-breasted cape-coat with draped collar by Pauline Trigère, **1959**; this designer is famous for her many versions of the cape.

Empire waistline and flare, combined with widened, cropped sleeve and collarless neckline started a new look in **1960**—adaptable for day or evening. This look was associated with Balenciaga and was typical of the simple, un-fussy clothes favored by the then First Lady, Jacqueline Kennedy.

In the sixties, coats were shorter and simpler. Fur trim and other details were out. Color and line were the most important features. Blanket plaid coat, **1962**, flares out from a stand-up collar that is very different from the lapels and portrait collars of the fifties. Short coat based on a sailor's pea jacket, **1962**, was by Saint Laurent, who was inspired by work clothes more than once.

1962

1962

1960

1965

1964

1967

1963

A **1963** bubble coat by Oscar de la Renta offered the contrast of a curving back and a smooth, plastron front.

At this time, the raincoat came into its own. It was no longer dowdy and purely utilitarian. The trenchcoat continued in many versions, from khaki poplin to black silk. In **1964**, this quilted raincoat with a satin finish started a trend. The quilted nylon raincoat, lightweight and washable, became a classic for travel and all-purpose wear. Long wool evening coat, **1965**, was cut as simply as a daytime style. (Five years later, the maxi coat had a brief success for daytime wear, but was quickly abandoned because the length proved impractical.) Beige canvas mini coat, **1967**, in pyramid silhouette, featured the giant industrial zipper closing known as the hardware look.

Another mini coat was styled like a bathrobe, in camel wool knit with piping, **1968**.

Fox-trimmed coat, **1970**, worn with fox hat, was inspired by the film, *Dr. Zhivago* and was considered a costume look at that time. By 1974, hemlines were dropping. The general easing of silhouettes was reflected in a loosening of coats.

The duffle is a constantly recurring theme; this version by Bill Haire for Friedricks, **1976**, was just right with casual pants or skirts.

Coat by Mrs. H. Winter for Yesterday's News, **1978**, had a shirred-sleeve shoulder treatment that foreshadowed wider shoulders of the 1980s.

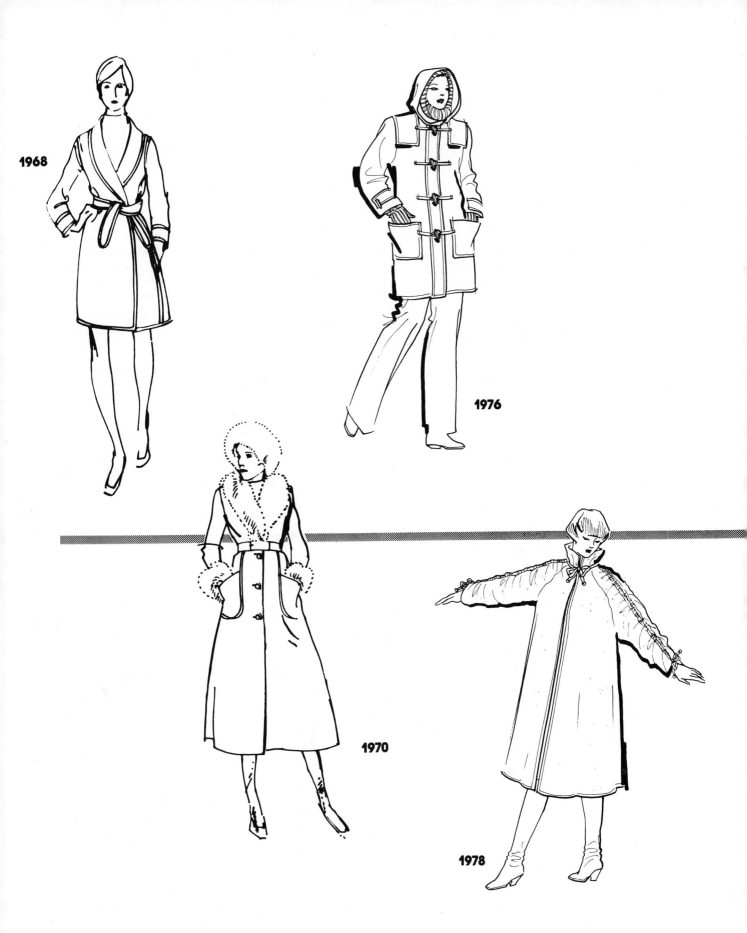

1968

1976

1970

1978

33

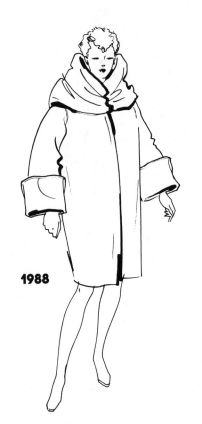

1988

By the late 1970s, lined trenchcoats and quilted down coats were basics for everyday wear; this continued through the 1980s. But coat designers were persistent, and turned out a choice of silhouettes.

Marc Bohan did a soft, wrappy coat with big, crushed collar for Christian Dior in **1988**.

Oscar de la Renta shaped a fitted coat, **1988**, with side-buttoning and architectural seaming.

Calvin Klein's **1989** coat, with its loose, swinging lines and deep armholes, could be worn over skirts or pants.

Karl Lagerfeld's full-length coat for Fendi, **1989**, was cut to ankle length. It recalled the maxi, but was softer, with fur buttons and fur lapels (shown turned up here).

1988

1989

1989

3

SUITS

The coat and suit industry was established in New York City at the turn of the century. In the 1890s there was what might be called a craft production industry located along lower Broadway. These houses, well known in their day, were forced out of business by what became known as "sweat shop" labor. The heads of these concerns retired with dignity to become bankers, wholesale cloth merchants or owners of department stores. Division Street was the center of the industry. Bundles of cut garments were taken over to the lower East Side to be manufactured in filthy tenements. These conditions caused many strikes and lockouts. The modern union probably should be dated and documented from the Protocol of Peace in 1910, which settled a nine-week strike in the needle industries of New York City.

1900

1913

1913

This early coat and suit industry depended on imported models bought in Berlin and Vienna, not in Paris. The department stores, however, bought models in Paris. These were displayed in the piece goods departments of the stores to be copied by the dressmakers. The **1900** model illustrated is of the latter type.

In the years that followed, the simple tailored suit, often bound with silk braid and worn with ruffled white blouses, became generally popular. We illustrate with an extreme example of the fitted suit worn in Paris in **1913**. This same year was known for the exaggerated dressmaker suits which seemed almost like dresses.

By **1923** the long-waisted style was accented by Poiret with a band of fur.

The vogue for ensembles was so strong in **1926** that even the suits took on these characteristics. The soft skirts had dressy overblouses with jackets lined to match the blouses.

By the 1930s America was back to simple suits with longer skirts. Many times the short jackets were of contrasting colors, **1936**.

In **1937** Schiaparelli was the first to use padding in the shoulders of women's suits. She borrowed the idea from the London Guardsman's uniform, which in turn was taken from the 15th century man's costume where these famous puffs were padding for armor.

1923

1926

1936

1937

1945

1947

1943

Adrian then developed this idea into the square-shouldered suit, **1943**, which was popular through the war years until 1947.

Very often in fashion when a new idea is born, it is some time before that idea is accepted. This was true of the so-called "New Look." In **1945** Balenciaga, following the traditions of his native Spain, showed a suit with padded hips and extremely small waistline, but the skirt was short.

In **1947**, Dior carried this idea further. He used the padded hip, but lengthened and widened the skirt, softened the shoulder and thus launched the New Look, with its attendant controversy. After the wartime restriction of fabric used in single garments, this new style was a welcome change.

The loosening of the rigid silhouette is apparent in bloused jackets and lightly padded natural shoulders for **1950**. The

cinched waist and close-to-body jackets were carried on with the impetus from the New Look until another significant fashion was launched by Balenciaga in **1954**. This, a semi-fitted jacket, was a startling change. The collar stood loosely away from the neck, the shoulder seams dropped, sleeves were shortened, the front of the jacket was lightly indented and the back was loose. This new concept of tailoring influenced on all designers.

A popular young style of suit was the princess line jacket and A-line skirt of **1955**, done in tweeds with sweater blouses for the college age group.

The second great suit influence of the fifties was that of Chanel. She made her comeback in 1954 and year after year showed new versions of her tailored, loose jacket with braid binding, combined with related blouses and costume jewelry. We show a **1958** version.

1954

1950

1955

1958

39

1960

1962

1959

1960

40

The rise of the sportswear market influenced every category of fashions. The mix-matching of separate skirts, tops and jackets became a new way to dress. The short pleated skirt and boyish blazer-type jackets worn with coordinated sweater blouses were mass fashions in **1959**.

In **1960**, the status suit was likely to be a vivid color—hot pink, turquoise, yellow or white—the unfitted short jacket, detailed with welt seaming, big, fancy crochet buttons and gathered peg-top skirt.

The increasing blending of smart country into town dressing brought tweeds into prominence by **1960**. The most prophetic town suit of that year was the culotte suit designed by Norman Norell, meant for sophisticated town wear rather than country walks or bicycling.

Norell's culotte suit was ahead of its time, but his **1962** suit, shown here, was an all-time classic. A gray wool clipped jacket combined with a gored, flared skirt, belted in patent leather, and a soft, bowed blouse of peach surah.

Tweed overblouse suit, **1963**, traded the conventional jacket for a pullover top. Again, the waistline was bypassed. White wool pantsuit, **1963**, by André Courrèges. This was one of his early designs. As a look for streetwear, it was ahead of its time. It was worn with the white leather boots that were an essential part of the Courrèges look. Balenciaga's **1964** bubble suit of fluffy tweed shows how the "master" sculptured his silhouettes. The jacket moves over the waistline without marking it, curves in back, and tapers in towards a narrow hemline. Balenciaga created clothes for women. The youth revolution was under way, and "womanly" looks were about to disappear, or, at least, to go out of fashion.

1964

1963

1963

1966

1968

A **1966** Ben Zuckerman suit combined three related parts: a camel jacket reversed to pinstriped fabric of the blouse; the skirt was camel.

John Anthony designed the gaucho suit in **1968**, with its full pants, long for an era of miniskirts. White crepe shirts and strictly tailored ties were signatures of this designer. By 1968, fashionable women were wearing pantsuits on the street, though they were still turned away from some fashionable restaurants! Jacques Tiffeau, a tailor in an era marked by the disappearance of tailors, posed a cape over a brief jumpsuit in **1968**.

Suits continued to merge with sportswear; separates were worn as suits. For fall, **1974**, Givenchy showed a tweed smock suit in the incoming silhouette. The somewhat wider shoulders were round and soft. The skirt, worn with boots, was cut to below-the-knee length.

A **1979** suit by Oscar de la Renta recalled the 1930s and 1940s, with its fitted and flared peplum jacket and pocket detailing.

More women wanted leather clothing every year; it was status fashion. We show a **1981** suit by Yves Saint Laurent; the long, bloused jacket over a short, narrow skirt was a silhouette that continued to develop through the decade.

1974

1979

1968

1981

43

1989

In the 1980s Giorgio Armani came up with new ideas about tailoring that influenced and changed suit design. Less construction, no fussy details, subtle, pared-down cuts and drapery were some characteristic Armani ideas. We show a **1989** Armani suit with long jacket over short, draped skirt.

By the late 1980s, shoulders were rounding and softening again. This **1989** coat-and-skirt suit by Bill Blass shows the incoming, rounded shoulder, and is still another version of long length over short length.

In **1989** Valentino Boutique updated the pantsuit. At that time, the pantsuit was undergoing a revival, after falling out of favor in the early 1980s. This Valentino design combined a cardigan jacket with easy, full trousers.

1989

1989

44

4

SPORTSWEAR

In 1900 what passed for active sportswear was hardly different from everyday clothing, so rigid were standards of modesty. Shirtwaist blouses and skirts, two of the first mass-produced separates, were an early fashion uniform of the century.

The 1920s was a period of liberation. It was then that "spectator sportswear" developed. Spectator sportswear referred to the informal, tailored clothing women wore when they attended tennis matches and golf tournaments—white pleated dresses and navy flannel jackets, for example. Active sportswear became sharply differentiated from everyday clothing as standards of modesty relaxed.

Sportswear as daytime wear had its roots in the 1930s. Designers like Schiaparelli showed knitted T-shirts as blouses to wear with tailored suits—a daring idea at the time. In the United States, a few designers with limited followings developed practical clothes. In New York, Elizabeth Phelps designed a denim wrap skirt that was copied decade after decade. However, the age of sportswear was still to come.

In the 1940s, Americans were cut off from the inspiration—and domination—of Paris. Designers like Tom Brigance, Bonnie Cashin, Tina Leser and Claire McCardell, among others, became famous for their new concepts of what casual clothing could be.

After the war, sportswear went international. There were French, Italian and British contributions, especially in knitwear. Leather coats and separates developed into a new category.

Casual sportswear fitted in with a new way of life in America: life in the suburbs. Many people moved to the suburbs during the 1950s. They entertained informally. They drove their children to school. They gardened and shoveled snow. The comfort and informality of sportswear met their needs.

Increased leisure time and higher income

levels created a middle-class society that traveled all over the world. Lightweight separates plus a good-looking raincoat added up to a practical travel wardrobe. The raincoat emerged as a new fashion category, closely related to sportswear.

Active sportswear also expanded during the fifties. More women took to such sports as skiing and scuba diving, while continuing to play traditional games such as tennis and golf.

The jeans of the youth revolution of the 1960s were a new separate that soon passed into the fashion mainstream. They were a sign of things to come; in 1970, uncertainty about skirt lengths turned women to pants for street wear. This was an important milestone in fashion history. From then on, women wore pants with blouses, jackets and sweaters for many daytime and evening occasions.

During the 1970s, and on through the 1980s, the sportswear influence was strong in daytime clothing. The separates of 1990 were a far cry from the shirtwaists and skirts of the early 1900s, but the appeal was the same—sportswear is informal, comfortable clothing that can be switched around and worn in different ways.

Pattern for a cardigan sweater, designed by Schiaparelli, **1939**, "for country tweeds, skating skirts or ski trousers." Wide shoulder, typical of the era, was accented by band of cable stitching down the sleeve.

Women wore peasant blouses and skirts in the 1940s. We show a ruffled cotton blouse and apron skirt, **1944**. The blouse has an elasticized neckline that can be pulled down and worn off the shoulder. The skirt is straight and not as full as the designer would have liked, because of wartime restrictions on the use of fabric. Wedgie shoes are a finishing touch.

Bare midriff top and tapered pants, Claire McCardell, **1944**, both of gray wool jersey. This designer was always ahead of her time—she anticipated the popularity of knits. Buttoning created the effect of shoulder width without padding.

1939

1944

1944

Plaid wool throw by Bonnie Cashin, **1946**. It was described as a "sort of stole" and preceded a wave of ponchos and stoles that continued through the 1950s.

By **1948**, sportswear showed the influence of Dior's "New Look." Camisole top is worn with matching stole. Skirt is quilted taffeta. Dressy accessories include looped rope of pearls, cummerbund sash, and ankle strap sandals.

Black leotard, tights and tweed jumper, **1955**, were associated with "beatnik" looks of the fifties, and became conventional sportswear of the sixties. Leisure wear became increasingly popular during the fifties. Emilio Pucci's silk jersey prints, vivid and abstract, influenced decades of sportswear. The tapered pants and overshirt are dated **1957**. Pucci's discreet signature on his printed fabrics set a trend that was eventually exaggerated.

1955

1946

1948

1957

49

1958

1959

1958

Sportswear separates combining a white permanently pleated skirt of washable fabric based on synthetic fibers and a flowered cotton jacket blouse were a city-country way of dressing from **1958** on.

Striped knit pullover and straight-leg white duck pants and sneakers, **1958**, were adopted by sailors ashore and afloat.

The growth of television inspired at-home dressing in two parts, for instance, cashmere sweaters with ankle-length mohair plaid skirts, **1959**.

One-piece jumpsuits were adopted for sports car driving as well as for flying, **1960**. Water skiing and skin diving increased towards the end of the fifties. Special rubberized one-piece suits provided protection against the cold.

Denim pants and a blue denim shirt were shown as casual sportswear in **1962**. The outfit was strictly for country wear, but the use of denim was significant.

Heavy, textured sweaters contrasted with slick, shiny black leather, **1962**.

The **1963** shirtdress of butterscotch suede was worn over a turtleneck sweater, another example of the idea of layering one piece of clothing over another. In a sense, the dress was used as a separate. In **1963**, African safari outfits inspired the safari shirt, with many pockets. It is shown here as a belted jacket over a black turtleneck sweater, with whipcord pants. This was still a leisure look, not a "street" look.

1960

1962

1962

1963

1963

51

1967

1964

1964

1967

52

Two Bonnie Cashin outfits, both dated **1964**, show how this designer expanded the scope of sportswear. For evening, black wool jersey dress teams with black leather coat. The coat collar is fluffy mohair knit, as casual as a sweater. Layered grouping of separates includes reversible pile-lined coat, hood, vest, wool jersey dress, all with signature leather piping.

By the mid-sixties sophisticated women were wearing trousers on the street. There were some alternatives to trousers, such as the knicker suit, **1967**, of pepper-and-salt tweed, worn with ribbed hose and flat-heeled shoes, a young look. Wheat-colored cashmere sweater is styled like a button-down shirt, **1967**. The sweater tucks into a wide belt over a gray wool chinchilla mini-skirt. This was one of the few belted looks of the late sixties, when the chemise was a uniform. Beige and gray was a favorite color combination.

Anne Klein was famous for putting together separates with an all-American dash and snappiness. Shown: her navy flannel blazer, gray flannel pants and white shirt, **1968**. This outfit was for street wear, as opposed to earlier pants for leisure wear. Anne Klein's sweater set was dated **1972**. It combined two different lengths, accented by border patterns.

Sonia Rykiel, a designer of French ready-to-wear, is especially famous for her sweater themes. For winter, **1975**, she offered a sweater with deep cape collar recalling the "Bertha" collars on soft crepe blouses of the twenties and thirties. The skirt is stitched down to pleated fullness. Rykiel has said that her customers can choose the length of their skirts, but this one seemed destined to hover over the ankles, as she showed it.

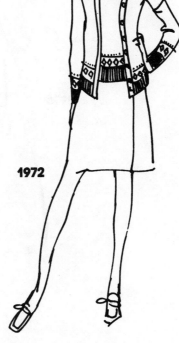

1975

1972

1968

The Rykiel and Klein designs are two of many examples of the expanding concept of sportswear, which can no longer be separated from other markets in the old-fashioned sense. White crepe blouse, **1975**, another style inspired by the soft blouses of the thirties, had inserts of faggotting. The crepe was nylon or polyester, rather than silk or rayon of earlier times.

The range of sportswear continued to expand during the late 1970s and all through the 1980s. Sportswear could be dressy or casual, or both dressy *and* casual, as in the crepe de chine trouser and tunic outfit designed by Kasper for J.L. Sport in **1976**.

Active sportswear themes translated easily into general sportswear, as in a **1976** design by Bill Haire for Friedricks; velvet jodphurs with a cashmere sweater. The idea of velvet, a dressy fabric, used for jodphurs, was typical of sportswear design.

Films influenced fashion: in **1977**, actress Diane Keaton starred in *Annie Hall* and created a new menswear look; oversized, relaxed, slightly rumpled and the very opposite of "dressed up." Yet it was not sloppy. Men's ties and hats were extra

1975

1976

1976

touches. The tie was knotted loosely and the hat was tilted or worn on the back of the head. The attitude was as important as the clothing itself.

By **1978**, Ralph Lauren was developing his western-inspired sportswear. We show one of his flounced prairie skirts, with a fringed leather jacket and a chambray blouse. Lauren combined low-key chic with romanticism; his clothes often had a suggestion of "old money" that many women found appealing. He revived interest in ladylike pearls and in Native American jewelry and other accessories.

Norma Kamali reveled in audacity and retro, though she, too, sometimes turned to active sportswear for inspiration, as in her **1981** flippy dress of cotton gauze. (Her sweatshirt separates were widely copied.)

Perry Ellis for Portfolio was the label of another outstanding designer of the 1970s and 1980s. We show a **1983** outfit of cropped, bulky sweater worn over a high-rise, flared skirt; the cable detail was one of his signatures.

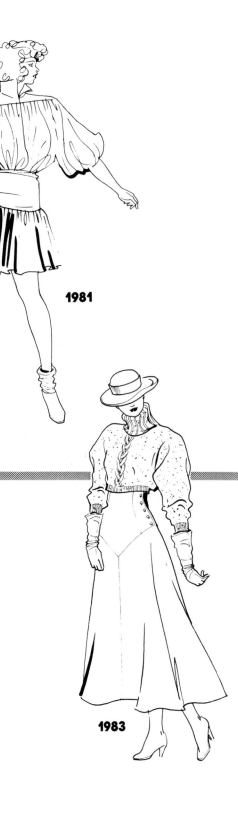

1981

1977

1983

1978

1985

1985

1985

1985

1989

In **1985**, Ellis showed a boyish outfit of layered sweater-jackets over close-fitting, cropped pants.

Calvin Klein is another designer who likes casual, easy shapes. We show a three-piece outfit, **1985**; loose coat of jacquard linen, worn with an easy-fitting blouse and full, cropped pants.

Norma Kamali's three-piece outfit, **1985**, was made of cotton sheeting. The cuffed pants, jacket and wide belt combined elements of the 1940s and 1950s. The leopard hat was made of printed fabric, not fur.

Donna Karan re-invented the bodysuit and used it as the basis for her layered looks, first, in black knit and later in colors and woven fabrics. We show a **1985** bodysuit, and full-length skirt with Karan's characteristic draping.

Rebecca Moses poised her long sweaters over leggings, **1989**. In this ultimate expression of "long over short" the skirt disappeared entirely. The dramatically leggy look ended in round-toed, short boots.

5

A C T I V E

S P O R T S W E A R

1943

More participation in sports is a by-product of women's liberation. Women have been swimming and playing tennis and golf for a long time; by 1990 they played with more skill. They also jog, run and work out in gyms. Girls have won the right to play on Little League baseball teams, formerly restricted to boys.

Though recognition of women's team sports has been slow, an older generation pioneered in professional baseball back in the 1940s, when World War II pulled men off teams and into the army.

We begin our active sportswear section by noting the All-American Girls Professional League that played from 1943 to 1954, and we show the uniform of the **1943** Racine Belles. The skirt was extremely short in its day.

Team or individual, amateur or professional, active sportswear has two functions. It allows for freedom of movement and it protects against the elements—sun, water, snow.

Another function developed over the years, women began to wear active sportswear, and adaptations of it, for all informal occasions. Tennis sweaters, ski sweaters and golf skirts became part of fashion.

In the late 1980s, women began to buy riding jackets, jodphurs and boots in shops that specialized in riding gear; they wore these clothes on the street.

This conversion of active sportswear into everyday clothing often had a quality of fantasy about it. If you dressed like a champion rider, or tennis player, or golfer, people might take you for a champion! Fantasy is always an important part of fashion.

Swimsuits are a special part of active sportswear. They are decorative as well as functional.

Swimming was one of the first active sports women took up at the beginning of the twentieth century.

B E A C H W E A R

Swimsuits are a special case. They are worn
for relaxing and sunning, a "passive" sport,
as well as for swimming. Swimsuits, more
than any category of clothing, tell the story
of changing standards of modesty from
1900 on.

The bathing suit of **1900** was of heavy wool
serge. One of the most popular styles of this
period was the sailor dress, the style of the
famous Peter Thomson being carried out in
the bathing suit.

The real turn of the century in bathing fashions came with the one-piece knit suit
which originated in Australia and was pop-
ularized by Annette Kellerman in **1910**.
This, according to press reports of those
days, was a shocker greater than the bikini
of the late forties.

1910

1900

1924

1930

1943

Covered legs persisted for many years, even with the slim, above-knee-length slip of a bathing dress worn in **1924**. While not so labeled at the time, this dress foreshadowed the "dressmaker" bathing dress that attained its height in the 1930s and 1940s, and which won a place of its own for the beach or playsuit as distinguished from the swimsuit.

In the 1930s, while dressmaker skill and detail were being developed in this feminine type of dress, the arrival in the market of elasticized yarns produced a new appraisal of the sleek one-piece maillot, **1930**. Both shared success for many seasons. The dressmaker suit we show is typical of **1943**, with its flared gored skirt. Curtailment of elasticized yarn halted production of this type of garment during World War II, but the bare midriff suit, followed by the two-piece (bra and shorts of brief skirt) aroused new interest. Brevity was the password in these suits, preparing the way for the French bikini of **1947**. With the end of the war the satin lastex maillot returned.

The strapless top of the late 1940s introduced corsetière techniques in beachwear. Wiring and boning made possible the built-in bra and form fitting shapes corresponding to the technique used in strapless evening gowns, as in our **1948** suit.

The swing of the pendulum moved toward the tube suit of knitted wool in **1950**.

After an interval of seven years, the two-piece suit was again popular, this time with little-boy shorts and built-up camisole bra in **1955**.

1955

1950

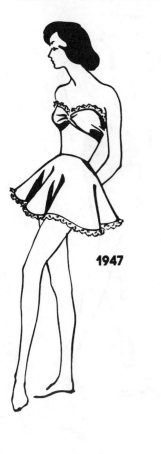

1947

1948

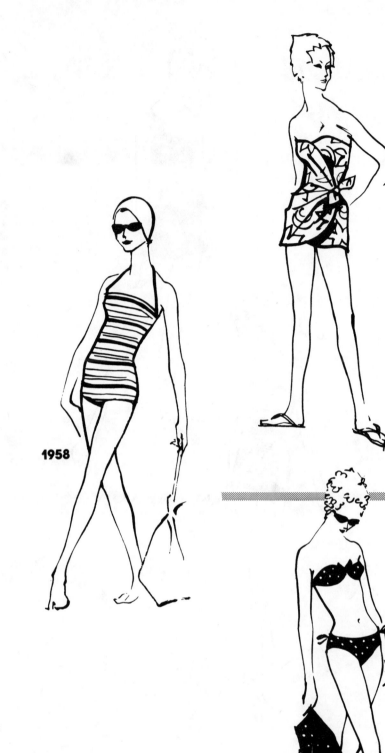

Later refinements in stretch yarns introduced the multistriped knit maillot, **1958**, with removable straps for even tanning of shoulders. The printed cotton dressmaker suit in one piece was very popular in Hawaiian prints in the sarong wrap style—big in **1959** and continuing into the sixties.

The brief bikini finally spread from Caribbean resorts across the United States in **1960**, first for private pools and, later, on public beaches.

The one-piece maillot in knit fabrics, usually black, became streamlined in 1959. It rose high and straight across in front and plunged deeply in back to expose a wide expanse for tanning.

The end of **1960** introduced a new relaxed soft suit, almost a bloused chemise of light jersey or silk with modest neckline and de-emphasis of molded bosom.

Broad stripes of red, white and blue were used horizontally or vertically on one-piece knit maillots. The ratio of one-piece to two-piece suits was nearly equal at the end of 1960.

1958

1959

1960

1960

By 1960, stores were beginning to find that women who bought swimsuits also wanted some kind of cover-up. This was especially important as suits became briefer. Covering was needed on the beach as a protection against too much sun. A skirt or top also carried the swimsuit from beach or poolside to a nearby restaurant or club for lunch.

Swimwear expanded into a larger category—beachwear. Many of the dresses and skirts worn on the beach soon appeared away from the beach because they were attractive and comfortable. Beachwear became at-home wear, informal evening wear, and even streetwear.

Mexican wool poncho, **1960**, a swimsuit cover or a lightweight wrap—a substitute for a sweater.

Striped cotton ticking dress, **1961**. Down-to-earth "homey" fabrics like ticking are often used for sportswear.

1961

1960

1960

1962

1964

1962

1964

1966

66

Scuba diving, a serious sport requiring skill and strength, called for practical suits like this one by Ernst Engel, **1962**. It is yellow vinyl, with zipper and long sleeves. In a more frivolous mood, the two-piece beach outfit by Micia, **1964**. This Italian designer cut "portholes" in the white jersey top and piped them in black, to match the bikini pants. (A good example of an imaginative beach outfit that didn't go in the water.)

In the sixties, Rudi Gernreich pioneered the simple, unconstructed wool tank suit—this, in an era when some suits were still lined and boned like evening gowns. For possessors of a good figure, the Gernreich suits were liberating. We show a striped **1962** version.

There were many more, some deeply cut-out. Gernreich's famous "topless" suit of **1964** created a scandal, but was prophetic.

Black wool suspenders formed a V that joined the trunks.

From 1965 on, beach fashions multiplied at an amazing rate. We show some styles of the 1965–68 period. Ruffled striped nightshirt dress, **1966**, was inspired by the film *Tom Jones*.

A jersey dress, **1966**, combines two different stripes and is worn with a dotted hat.

Two-piece outfit combining long "Nehru" tunic with mandarin-like collar, and white sharkskin pants, **1967**.

A beach dress—or at-home dress—or evening dress—in an African cotton print, **1967**: one of many fashions that grew from the theme "Black is Beautiful."

1967

1966

1967

1967

1967

1973

Another beach cover-up of **1967** was the short white nylon caftan with attached hood. Three-color cotton knit tank dress, **1967**, from St. Tropez, the famous French resort, where many fashions started.

Beachwear designs multiplied, but swimsuit design lagged. By 1970, there were still three basic suit types. There was the constructed one-piece suit, modestly cut, with inner bust cups and inner panties. Sometimes it had a skirt. There was the two-piece suit, modest or daring. There was an unconstructed maillot, or one-piece suit, suitable only for women with slim figures.

Few designers specialized in swimsuits over a long period of time. One of the few was Tom Brigance. We show one of his **1973** outfits, three pieces in an interesting red-and-white geometric print. The top combines halter and bra styling. The pants are unseen here, covered by a long skirt that converts the suit into a two-piece dress.

The string suit, **1974**, was an even briefer version of the bikini.

By the end of the 1970s, there were topless beaches and nude beaches, but these were still exceptions to the rule.

Suits remained brief and revealing. In the 1980s, designers cut suits high on the leg, down and out at back, front and sides. Stretch fabrics assured second-skin fit. During the late 1980s there was a move towards the one-piece suit, often very much cut out.

We show three **1988** styles.

The strapless Dior print, with its princess lines and skirt, recalls suits of the 1940s. The cap-sleeved, ribbed knit suit by Jantzen Jrs. has Empire seaming. A maillot with T-shaped, cut-out back is from JAG, Los Angeles.

The Anne Klein suit, **1989**, has a draped, sweetheart neckline, another reminder of the 1940s and 1950s.

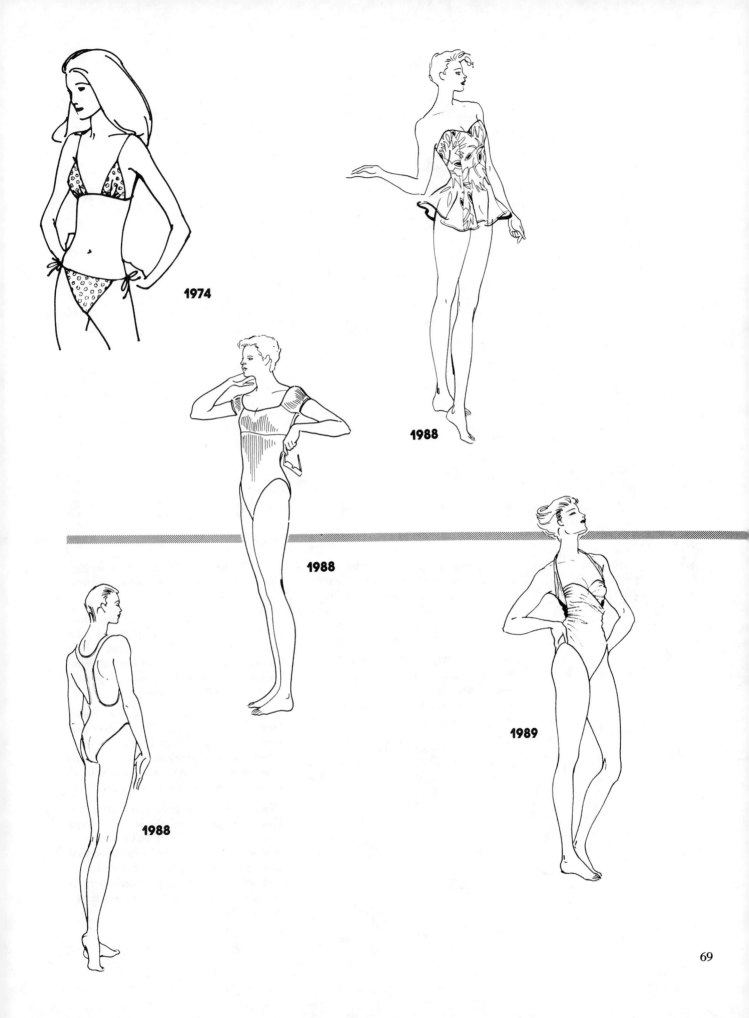

1974

1988

1988

1988

1989

T E N N I S

In **1900** women played tennis but it must have been a different game from the tennis matches. Their skirts were gored, barely clearing the ground, and they wore hats and rather fussy blouses. The only concession was a pair of tennis slippers or sneakers.

After World War I, Suzanne Lenglen, the French tennis star, had a specially designed tennis dress—sleeveless, skirt to the knee—made of white silk. With this she wore a silk band wrapped around her head. Our version is from **1921**. Spectacular for her wardrobe on the courts as well as for her tennis, she awakened the public to the sense, along with the chic, of a specialized kind of tennis dress. Helen Wills followed with a similar style made of cotton broadcloth with pleats in the skirt.

Alice Marble was the first to introduce shorts at the important tennis tournaments, **1946**.

The short tennis dress held its popularity though shorts, slacks and playsuits were also worn. In 1949, the American, Gussie Moran, made tennis fashion news at Wimbledon by wearing lace trimmed panties under her short tennis dress.

During the fifties tennis costumes remained fairly classic, always white, either with pleated skirt button front **1947** or a beltless princess dress. For informal games the all-white shorts and cotton knit polo shirt or sleeveless blouse were an alternative.

News often came from England where Teddy Tinling livened the all-white dress with feminine touches of colored embroidery or bands of lace at hems. He added white sweaters or jackets with matching embroidered emblems for after-tennis in the late fifties. We show a lace-hemmed dress, **1960**.

1900

1960

1946

1921

1947

71

1974

From the 1960s on, tennis clothing did not change significantly.

Gradually, insistence on all-white outfits diminished. In 1974, champion Billie Jean King wore a white dress with panels of color. We show a **1974** style with inserts of colorful cotton patchwork and a matching patchwork racket case. Our **1974** three-some of stretch terry has knitted bands and is influenced by the sweatshirt, a sports-wear classic. It was a typical informal costume on the courts and was also worn for other sports such as jogging.

The trend towards casual, comfortable shorts and skirts continued during the 1980s. In **1988**, champion Chris Evert wore this white camisole dress, trimmed with red piping.

1974

1988

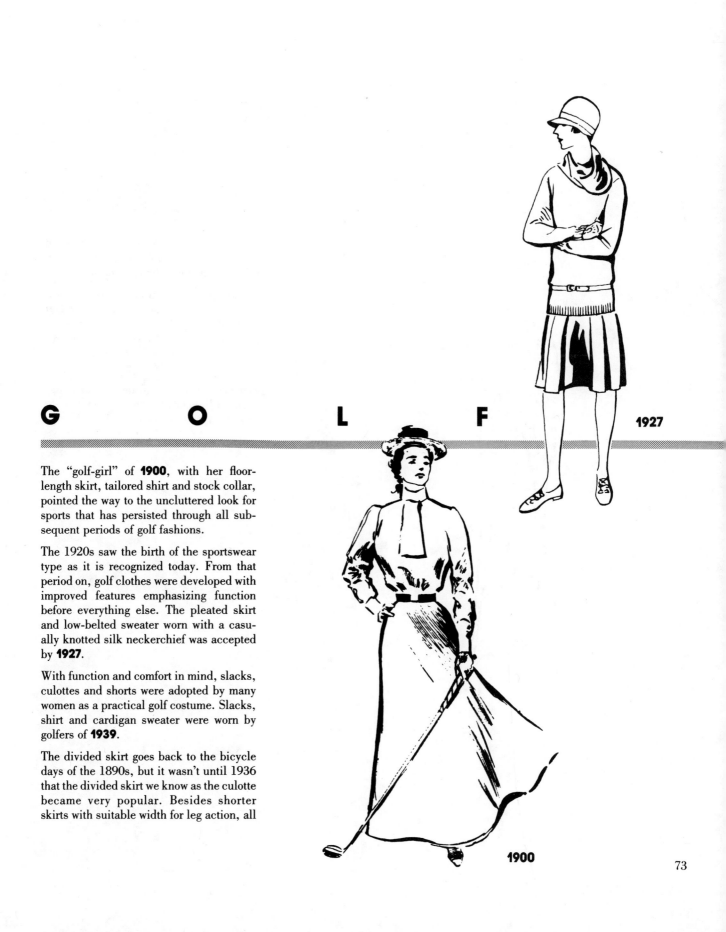

G   O   L   F

The "golf-girl" of **1900**, with her floor-length skirt, tailored shirt and stock collar, pointed the way to the uncluttered look for sports that has persisted through all subsequent periods of golf fashions.

The 1920s saw the birth of the sportswear type as it is recognized today. From that period on, golf clothes were developed with improved features emphasizing function before everything else. The pleated skirt and low-belted sweater worn with a casually knotted silk neckerchief was accepted by **1927**.

With function and comfort in mind, slacks, culottes and shorts were adopted by many women as a practical golf costume. Slacks, shirt and cardigan sweater were worn by golfers of **1939**.

The divided skirt goes back to the bicycle days of the 1890s, but it wasn't until 1936 that the divided skirt we know as the culotte became very popular. Besides shorter skirts with suitable width for leg action, all

1927

1900

kinds of individual devices in bodices and sleeves to ensure completely free action were designed to define golf fashion.

The mature woman still preferred the classic golf dress in monotone striped or checked cotton, **1948**. On cooler days she wore the easy flared flannel skirt and tailored man's shirt or sweater joined by striped webbing belt.

Younger athletes liked the ease and simplicity of Bermuda length shorts in linen or wool, worn with the new classic McMullen

1939

1948

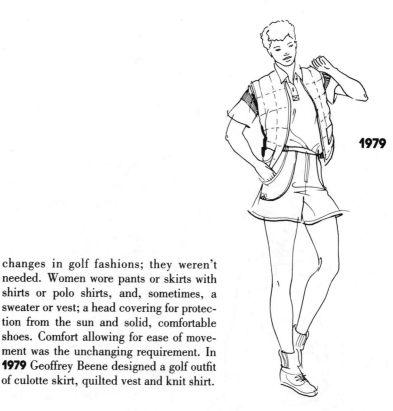

1979

cotton blouse, **1954**. Indian madras plaids were a fad throughout the 1950s worn as shorts, as long pants or as boyish jackets for after-game. Both men and women—especially college age—approved this fashion.

Toward **1960** a popular look on the golf course was the straight leg slacks worn with open neck cotton shirt and a boy's V-neck wool sweater, the head tied up in folded kerchief.

In the 1970s and 1980s there were no sharp changes in golf fashions; they weren't needed. Women wore pants or skirts with shirts or polo shirts, and, sometimes, a sweater or vest; a head covering for protection from the sun and solid, comfortable shoes. Comfort allowing for ease of movement was the unchanging requirement. In **1979** Geoffrey Beene designed a golf outfit of culotte skirt, quilted vest and knit shirt.

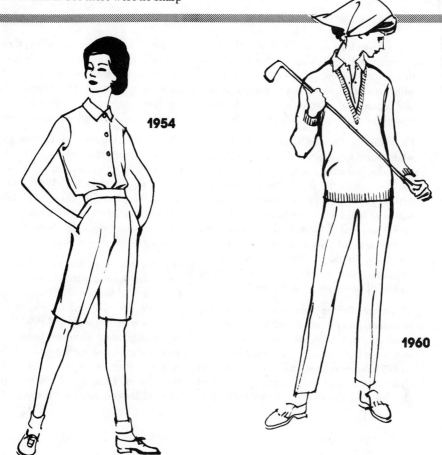

1954

1960

1900

R I D I N G

The side-saddle riding habit was the predominant riding fashion of **1900**. Early in this century women participated in sports with greater abandon and sportsmanship and began to adopt trousered and otherwise masculine fashions for riding astride.

First was the divided skirt of circular cut which came to the ground with a panel that was buttoned after dismounting to conceal the division in the front. Riding breeches with high boots or puttees and long jacket reaching to the knees composed the popular riding habit of **1916**. In this costume the jacket was of the same fabric as the breeches. In the 1930s jodhpurs gained popularity and tweed jackets were worn with twill breeches or jodhpurs.

There are stricter rules for dress among horsemen and women than for other participant sports. Hence the small change over the years from the classic look illustrated in **1931**. Formal hunt attire is so regulated that every fold of the cravat, the angle of the hat and the design of the buttons is prescribed. For informal riding, more color and individuality comes into the costume— the ratcatcher shirt and jodhpurs with head bound in a kerchief or the plaid jacket over a yellow vest with rust jodhpurs were early examples of informal riding clothes.

The 1940s brought a new, completely informal style of riding clothes—the Western rig—mainly characterized by Levis, cotton shirt and casual jacket, **1947**. Slim fitting frontier pants, silk shirt and elaborately trimmed jacket were one version of western style for dress wear. Levis were the tough-wearing pants of the Gold Rush days.

In riding habits, as with other active sportswear, the development of synthetic stretch fibers led to fabrics that hugged the body closely yet allowed for the necessary freedom of movement. In **1990**, formal riding outfits have slimmer pants, and the jacket may be shaped a little differently, with less flare below the waist. Otherwise, there is no category of clothing that has showed less change over the years.

1916

1947

1931

1990

77

1908

S K I I N G

Ski fashions played a minor role in the sportswear story until the 1950s.

The long-skirted fashions of **1908** were abandoned when "trousers in public" became an established fashion. Riding breeches and knickers were the first trouser styles adopted by women for ski costumes. These were worn with heavy sweaters and knee-length heavy socks. In the **1930s**, a ski suit was introduced with long, full trousers and jacket of the same fabric. The trousers and stretch pants of modern ski-wear look far more trim and practical than the bloused costume of the thirties.

The influences of "after-ski" wear have been far flung in all classes of fashion, from the embroideries and knitwear of the Tyrol to specialized footwear.

After World War II the ski craze swept the United States. Many Swiss and Austrian instructors opened resorts in the East and Colorado and introduced professional "downhill" streamlined pants, **1947**, identical for women and men. These pants became even more skin tight and flexible with the advent of stretch yarns around 1956. Solid black or navy suits gave way to much color on the slopes from 1955 on. The Eskimo hooded parka with long-haired fur on the inside started the bulky top-heavy look. Norwegian patterned sweaters and caps were a natural fad as were tremendous fox hoods and mittens. Lightweight nylon windproof fabrics developed for Polar expeditions were adopted by skiers. Quilted nylon hooded jackets became the most popular choice by **1959**. Tops and bottoms in brilliant, contrasting colors were fashionable for a while, but the trend towards monochromatic color schemes appears again in 1960 among expert skiers. The **1966** outfit reflects the chemise silhouette of its time.

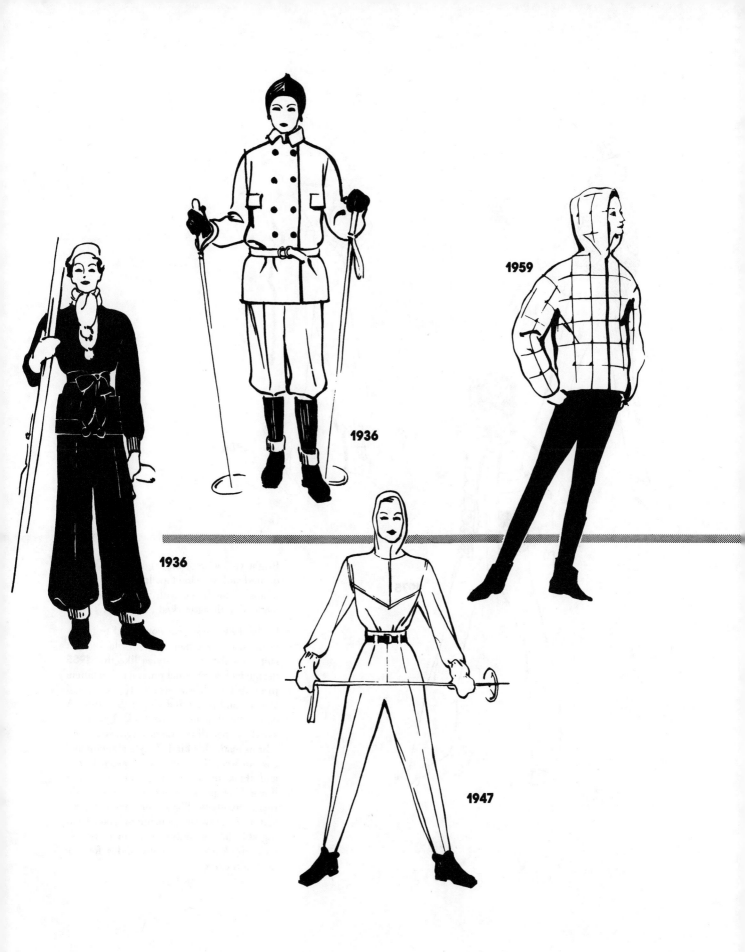

1936

1936

1959

1947

79

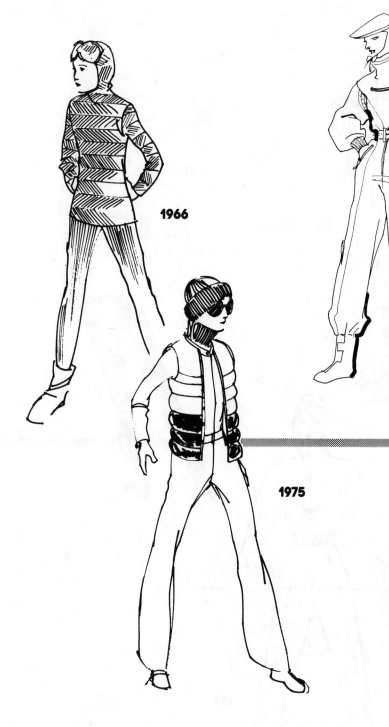

1966

1985

1975

Bright yellow wool knit tights team with a quilted yellow nylon top. In **1975**, a poplin jumpsuit combined with a vest in shaded tones of quilting worked circularly.

In the 1980s, skiwear continued to follow fashion, but was more varied. Sleek, tight suits co-existed with styles like this **1985** design by Peter Steinebronn, a nylon taffeta jumpsuit with sweater cuffs, bloused sleeves and pants and zipper detailing. A cap with attached scarf tucked into the stand-up neckline. Lightweight synthetic fabrics made this kind of style graceful and easy to wear; it would have looked lumpy and thick in the heavy wools of earlier times. The quick-drying properties of fabrics of synthetic fibers were another good feature for skiwear. Demand for good-looking ski clothes continued as more people took up skiing as a hobby and a form of healthful exercise.

1900

1916

S K A T I N G

1926

The **1900** skating girl moved across the ice in her "short" skirt, which showed more of her feet than any other skirt she wore.

The most conspicuous changes in skating fashions are evident in the shift of the skirt lengths illustrated by the costume worn at Tuxedo Park in **1916**.

In **1926**, when all skirts were shorter, the skating skirt hit knee level.

The great success and popularity of the skating star, Sonja Henie, gave figure skating a prominent place in the sports program. Influenced by her beautiful skating spectacles, the skating costume became more elaborate and decorative, the skirt shorter (the more expert the skater, the shorter the skirt), and the one-piece skating dress gained popularity.

The skating dress or skirt (worn with little jackets, sweaters or shirts) has a definite place in the story of active sportswear.

From **1947** on through the fifties the abbreviated skating dress was not replaced for exhibition skating. The only change was from flesh colored tights to black or red cotton tights which became a fad during the middle 1950s. These tights, borrowed from the ballet practice costume, were worn under tweed jumper dresses by school children as well as by working women for all-day winter wear.

Amateur skaters on city and country rinks wore the same stretch ski pants and bulky layers of sweaters worn for other winter sports.

The sport of skating took second place to the more popular skiing. In the late fifties, nylon stretch tights replaced earlier cotton tights. In 1975, skaters' gear ranged from brief dresses to sweaters with skirts or with jeans, those all-purpose pants that seem to be at home everywhere. The classic brief skirt seems quite conventional in the wake of micro-minis that were worn on the street in the late sixties and again in the nineties.

From the 1970s on, amateur and professional events aroused interest in competitive skating. But television turned skating into a spectator sport as millions of viewers tuned in to the winter Olympics. In **1989**, the "cat suit" unitard of stretch fabric, layered over a T-shirt, was a typical skaters' outfit.

1947

1989

6

YOUTH LOOKS

Before the youth revolution of the 1960s, girls copied women's clothes. Then came the great change; girls invented and women copied! This change in direction continued, and youth looks became an important source of mainstream fashion ideas.

These looks sometimes derived from unexpected combinations, like velvet and denim, or ruffles and leather.

Another characteristic was a reverence for the old, the used, the shabby and the antique. Jeans were worn to tatters, or were cut out, patched, frayed or fringed.

Some youth looks contradicted others. There were see-through effects, bareness, and skin-tight fit. But young girls—and boys—could also wear big, oversized jackets and thick, clunky shoes. Sometimes these contradictory ideas combined in one outfit, and created yet another look.

Fashion is always full of contradictions, and youth looks have expressed this theme in new, dramatic ways.

Tiered gypsy dress, **1969**, of crushed velvet, worn with wide belts, chains and jangling costume jewelry. "Hot pants" were a

1969

84

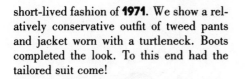

1971

1972

short-lived fashion of **1971**. We show a relatively conservative outfit of tweed pants
and jacket worn with a turtleneck. Boots
completed the look. To this end had the
tailored suit come!

Work clothing was a recurring theme.
Denim overalls, **1972**, plus a cotton print
blouse, with white collar and cuffs.

The bulky fisherman's knit sweater in off-
white knit with border trim, **1972**. It was a
winter coat, worn with other sweaters and
jeans. The heavy sweater as a coat was high
fashion by 1974.

1972

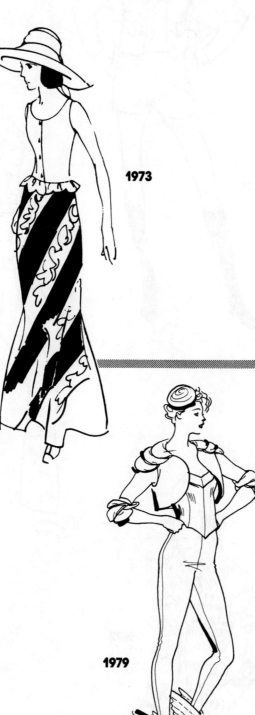

1973

The St. Tropez skirt hit in **1973**. It was made of spiraling panels of cotton, sometimes in two prints. It is shown with an antique corset cover blouse and a picture hat—typical touches of nostalgia. Such skirts were also worn with T-shirts and tailored shirts.

A roller disco outfit; **1979**, satin stretch bodysuit and tiny jacket in neon bright colors. With it, a tiny side-tilted hat and skate shoes with quilted "wings." This outfit, with pumps or sandals instead of skates, could have gone dancing in a disco.

From the beach at St. Tropez, **1981**, a sailor dress with old-fashioned middy collar, in white with navy trim.

Madonna, the famous singer and actress, went through many fashion phases. In **1985**, she wore lacy bras as outerwear, and

1979

1981

layered, see-through petticoats over tights. Young girls adopted these ideas enthusiastically.

The mid-1980s saw a revival of the mini. New styles were different from the styles of the 1960s; they were ultra-tight as well as ultra-short, thanks to stretch fabrics. We show a dress of puckered stretch fabric, **1988**, worn with a wide leather belt slung low at the waist.

A three-piece mini outfit, **1988**, with western pocket and stitching detail on cropped jacket, shirt and skirt. Concho-type belt is another Western accent.

In the summer of **1988**, young women wore short shorts on the street, choosing accessories that added to their individual fashion statements. A combination of cuffed shorts, shrug jacket and T-shirt was typical.

1988

1988

1985

1988

1989

1989

In **1989** bicycle pants were a fashion with several lives. For messengers speeding through city streets on bikes, they were work clothing. For health enthusiasts, they were exercise clothing. For young women who liked the sleek, revealing fit of stretch fabrics, they were a street look.

In **1989**, young people slashed their jeans at the knees, then made individual fashion statements (or anti-fashion statements!) by inventing cut-out patterns, frayed and fringed effects. We show cut-out jeans over socks worn with muffler, short jacket and long-sleeved T-shirt.

7

H   A   I   R

Hair is a unique accessory. Nature provides it but fashion dictates its arrangement. Hair can be a symbol of liberation or suppression. Between 1910 and 1915, the Irene Castle bob shook the world. Families shunned daughters who bobbed their hair—such girls were "fallen women." Yet in the 1960s short hair became a symbol of the establishment, of everything old-fashioned and "square." Young people wore their hair long and loose, as if it were a flag or a declaration of independence. When certain politicians spoke of "long-hairs," they spoke with contempt. Hairstyles have always veered from short to long and back again.

The Gibson Girl, **1900**. She wore a pompadour. She "put up" her long hair in back and combed front hair high off the forehead. Sometimes a "rat" or "switch" of hair or artificial padding filled out the pompadour. We show a choker and long necklace of genuine pearls, which a rich lady would have worn at that time.

The **1926** shingle was a severe, clipped version of short hair. It was slicked close

1900

1926

to the head and often worn with dramatic pendant earrings. The top of the head was flat, even when side hair was softer. Early permanent waves, or "perms" as they were called, could turn straight hair into frizz. Straight or curly, short hair was one of the most significant symbols of women's liberation.

After 1920, women began to wear cosmetics openly. They "painted" their faces with lipstick, powder and rouge. They applied makeup in public, just as they smoked and drank in public. The older generation was shocked.

In **1934**, Jean Harlow's platinum blond curls flashed across the silver screen. Women bleached their hair to this new, almost-white shade. Hair was longer. The style we show here was popular—smooth top, breaking into curls that just cleared the shoulder. Some women had permanent waves on the "half head" or the "ends." Others wore deeply-ridged fingerwaves or marcel waves. Bleached or dyed hair was still considered "fast," and the colors were harsh and unnatural. Bright red lipstick,

rouge and nail polish were popular. Eyebrows were plucked thin. Some women plucked off the natural brow entirely and penciled in an artificial brow.

The page boy, **1938**; one of the most popular styles of all times. Hair was still smooth on top, parted at center or side. It swung out freely and was turned under at the ends, but not rolled tightly or pinned. This was an ideal style for women with straight or slightly wavy hair. The page boy covered the ears. Small side combs or bobby pins above the ears were supposed to be invisible.

The pompadour, **1940**, was very different from the Gibson Girl style of 1900. In 1940, long hair was an inch or so below the shoulders—not waist-length as in 1900. Front hair was combed up off the forehead and pinned under, but no inside padding was used. Back hair could be pinned up, as shown here, or it could fall into a page boy. Our model wears a thin velvet ribbon choker. (Chokers are one of those fashions that appear again and again throughout the history of fashion.)

1940

1938

1934

1953

1964

In the forties, women wore bright and dark red lipstick. Powder and rouge were sometimes worn over a foundation known as "pancake" makeup. Society debutantes and film stars continued to inspire fashions in hair and makeup as well as in clothing.

The pixie cut, **1953**. Audrey Hepburn was one of the film actresses associated with this short, curly hairstyle. It created a small head, an idea that came in with the New Look of 1947. Tendrils of hair framed the face and curled down the nape of the neck. It is interesting to contrast this style with the clipped, severe shingle of 1926— another small head look.

By 1950, permanent waves had improved and there were new methods of setting hair. Makeup also changed. Pale, almost white lipsticks replaced the bright red shades. Eye makeup was worn during the day as well as in the evening. Eyebrows were more natural and less plucked. Slightly longer "Italian" curls were also worn. They were casual, almost ragged—completely differ-

ent from the precise, tight lines of earlier years.

The teased bouffant, **1964**. This is a short version. Many were longer, with fullness at the sides as well as on top of the head.

When long hair was teased up and pulled back, it was known as a "beehive." Teasing was not a new idea, but it was very popular during the sixties and persisted into the seventies. During the sixties, women wore hairpieces and wigs openly. Hair became more of an accessory then ever. Dyeing and bleaching processes were much improved, so that a far more subtle range of colorings was available. Hair coloring was no longer something to do secretly. It was just another aspect of fashion. Hair, sprayed to keep it firmly in place, took on a hard, rigid look. All this teasing and spraying finally killed hats. Women who spent time and money creating a silhouette of hair would not hide and crush it under a hat.

Long, straight hair, **1964**, was a youth sym-

1964

1967

bol of the decade; a uniform for young women who wore jeans, avoided makeup and scorned the idea of teasing and spraying. The difference between our two 1964 illustrations expresses the mood of the youth revolution and the division between generations.

The status pull, **1967**. Not all women teased their hair. Some pulled it back and tied it with a silk scarf, preferably one "signed" by a famous designer. This was a casual, sporty fashion—a sort of "society lady" look that was much imitated.

The Afro, **1968**. Black women enhanced the natural qualities of their hair, instead of straightening it. The height and width of early Afros paralleled the height and width of bouffant styles. Later, shorter versions of the Afro were known as "naturals." Long earrings, like the wire hoops we show, were worn with Afros and naturals.

Young black women turning towards their African ancestry for fashion inspiration, re-

1968

1972

discovered the corn row. We show a **1972** version. The corn row was really a form of sculpture. Hair was parted and braided on and off the head to form shapes. The hair was controlled by oiling, but not straightened. Tremendous variety was possible—every woman could do her own thing. Good bone structure helped. Cosmetics geared to black complexions followed the new hairstyles, filling a serious gap. Powder, especially, had been a problem. "White" powders tended to give black complexions a grayish cast.

By **1975**, waves of fashion nostalgia affected hair as they affected clothing. Our softly waved coiffure recalls the thirties; the softness makes the difference. While most makeup was natural-looking, some women took to "painting" their lips and cheeks bright red, proving again that fashion often looks back as it moves forward.

1975

1980s

In the 1980s, many film and television stars inspired complicated arrangements of long hair that looked spontaneous and unplanned, and even dishevelled, by standards of other years. But these arrangements called for careful planning and, sometimes, permanent waves. Curls and waves mixed with straight hair; tendrils fell over the face.

Many women preferred shorter cuts, simply waved over the ears, stopping just above the shoulder.

In **1989**, there was a sudden vogue for short hair. Now hair was straight or slightly waved and clipped at a level just below the ear. We show a typical style; the young woman wears small glasses, reminiscent of the granny glasses of the 1960s that were coming back into fashion.

Black women continued to wear versions of the "natural" that were clipped very short or allowed to grow out for a softer look. Young black women took to another African-inspired style that involved long, tight braids, intertwined with beads.

In 1988, young black women—and men—took to the "fade." Sides were clipped short while the top was cut straight across, as in old-style crewcuts. Later, there were variations; sometimes the sides were graduated from totally shaven up to a slight growth. In another version, the straight top layer was turned into waves. This was one style that could not be worn by anyone with limp hair!

Throughout the 1980s, inventive ways of wearing hair seemed like a substitute for hats. The hair stylist was a mysterious, powerful person, as the hat designer had been fifty years earlier.

1980s

1989

8

H A T S

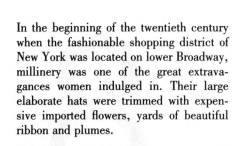

1900

1900

In the beginning of the twentieth century when the fashionable shopping district of New York was located on lower Broadway, millinery was one of the great extravagances women indulged in. Their large elaborate hats were trimmed with expensive imported flowers, yards of beautiful ribbon and plumes.

The Gibson Girl of **1900** wore a small trimmed hat placed forward on the head and a sailor hat for tailored and sportswear. By **1903** the automobile necessitated the addition of a chiffon veil, sometimes worn over the face, to keep out the clouds of dust. The hat was always securely tied down. Reminiscent of the Merry Widow is the large hat with the willow plum of **1910**.

This was also the era of the mesh face veil worn with tailored hats trimmed with wings,

1903

1912

1913

1910

quills or bows of ribbon. In **1912** the toque was introduced as a very small hat, but it seems large and clumsy in contrast with the more modern type of **1913**.

By **1919** the flat-brimmed, small-crowned, trimmed models were worn with dressy, soft afternoon costumes.

The 1920s brought in simple untrimmed dresses, accompanied by untrimmed hats. The cloche became the uniform of every woman. Varying in the material used and in manipulation, it was always worn well down over the eyes.

Expressing this same simple tendency were the untrimmed brimmed hats worn with soft silk afternoon dresses.

Increasing interest in spectator sports clothes led to the development of the simple sport hat of felt or straw. Reboux was the big name in the twenties. Her "Gigolo" crown, irregularly crushed in, was a highlight of **1925**. Rose Descat was a leader in the late twenties and thirties making the molded crown and eye-shading brim of the cloche a universal fashion teamed with close, shingled hair and smooth forehead. A soft-brimmed hat of **1931** complements the softer, more feminine bias-cut fashions of the time.

The basic simple shapes of the "calot" or "beanie" and the small squared pillbox became popular with the page boy bob and longer hair. We show a pillbox tilted to the side, **1934**, and a calot set back on the head, **1936**. The Duchess of Windsor's back-of-the-pompadour hat from Suzanne Talbot had a wide influence in 1936–37.

1936

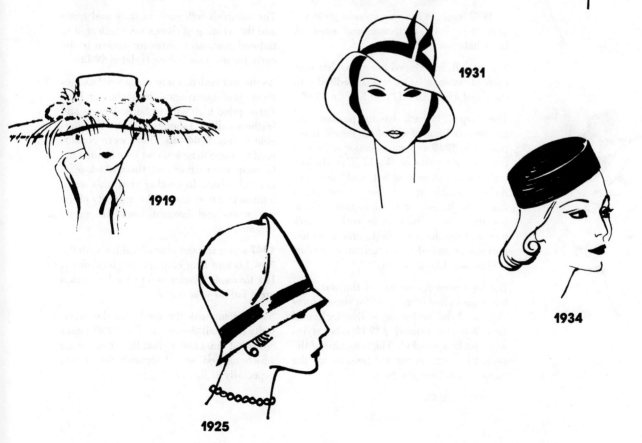

1919

1931

1934

1925

1939

1942

1941

1937

1938

In **1937** the halo hat was seen in great variety from small to tremendous sizes. A large halo hat is shown.

Schiaparelli introduced her clown hat with pointed crown in 1936, and is credited with the tiny forward tilted "doll hat" in **1938**.

The draped turban, having perhaps the greatest tradition of any of the forms, reappeared in **1939** and was a major style during the four years of World War II. The turban was a glamorous hat, and, in a more down-to-earth incarnation, symbolized Rosie the Riveter of wartime fame. Rosie was the woman who went to work in a factory to help the war effort, and wore her hair safely tucked into a turban, or a scarf tied to look like a turban.

But hats were a casualty of the war. The vogue for hats of fabric, and for snoods foreshadowed the beginning of the decline of hats. We show a snood of **1941**; other styles were made of crochet. The long hair of the period was caught up and held inside the snood, away from the face.

The mannish influence in suits and coats and the wearing of slacks were reflected in tailored mannish fedoras for women in the early forties. Our fedora is dated **1942**.

As the war ended, there was a brief excitement over extravagant hats coming from Paris, piled high with ribbons, flowers and feathers called "Liberation" hats. Fashionable during **1944–45**, these were considered by some to be a secret joke against the German occupation and their black-market-rich wives. In another view, this was a natural reaction against the austerity of the war years and brought back the pretty trimmed hat.

1947 was a vintage year in fashion with the New Look of Dior emphasizing femininity. His tiny side placed beret in velvet was a great fad all year round.

Sally Victor took the credit for the popularity of the all-flower hat. Her **1950** *Vogue* cover hat launched a great flower sequence which carried on all through the fifties, especially at Easter.

1944

1950

1952

1947

1955

1958

1959

Massed flowers in "wig" hats, tall toques, bandeaus or wide brimmed hats were the badge of the American club-woman.

Another universal fashion starting around 1952 was the veiling hat, designed to control but not hide the newly important hairdos. This bit of veiling and appliquéd trim became a serious threat to milliners. The growth of the hairdressers' art conspicuously curtailed the buying of hats in the late fifties.

The tiny "half" hat of **1952** was a compromise style. The "cage" of veiling was another compromise. We show a **1955** cage with appliquéd velvet bows. Givenchy's tiny "chignon" hats became a high fashion in **1958**, coinciding with the smoothed back chignon or French twist hairstyle.

The Davy Crockett fur hats worn by children in 1955 anticipated more sophisticated fur hats for women. We show a typical fox hat, **1959**. All kinds of bushy furs, fake or real, and minks and sables were popular winter headgear.

1960

1966

1967

1966

1970

The First Lady, entering her first year in the White House in **1960**, sparked interest in pillboxes worn far back on thick short hair.

As we follow millinery from the lavish creations of the early 1900s to the tiny bits of fabric and veiling of the 1950s, the trend is clear. Hats continually lost ground as a major accessory. During the fifties, the new suburban way of life was not sympathetic to hats. Who could drive a car in a veil? Who would garden seriously in a feathered hat? By the sixties, bouffant hairstyles sounded another note of doom. When Courrèges introduced hats as part of his total look in the mid-sixties, they were not accepted, though his boots and gloves were. It was a sign of the times.

A few hats did find limited acceptance during the sixties. They were optional chic, rather than an essential part of chic, as they had been in earlier eras. Two millinery designers, Adolfo and Halston, later turned their talents to custom fashion and ready-to-wear. We show two Adolfo hats. First, the tasseled fez, **1966**. Adolfo's fedora, **1966**, has proved durable. The film, *Bonnie and Clyde* inspired a crocheted cloche, **1967**.

By **1970**, black women were wearing turbans inspired by African clothing. Starting with an oblong of cloth, usually printed cotton, each woman draped and tucked a style to suit her own taste. Some were high and elaborate, others were low and fairly simple, Batik cottons were often used. These dramatic turbans were very different from the mass-produced little wool jersey styles sold in stores. Turbans are a constantly recurring millinery theme. So are berets. Berets were never out, but in **1975**, they were suddenly fashionable again, worn many ways. We show a beret pulled down over the hair like a round, soft cap.

During the 1980s, there was talk of a revival of hats, but it was wishful thinking. Occasionally, women wore hats as a finishing touch. More often, they covered their heads for protection against weather. The summer straw was an attractive and practical accessory. But the mystique of the hat, the idea of the hat as a glamorous, frivolous, essential accessory that could charm and enchant—that did not return.

We show a wide-brimmed straw hat, **1985**, and a dashing leather hat by Michelle Jaffe, **1989**.

1989

1975

1985

103

9

F U R S

1900

Fur was used as a protection against the cold as far back as we have any record of civilization, but the fur coat as we know it today was born in the twentieth century. In **1900**, Alaska seal was the leading fur for daytime wear, but it was heavy in weight, stiff and boardy. For this reason some women preferred short coats. The little fur capes, tippets and tiny round muffs were worn with their cloth coats.

In the early part of the twentieth century softer coats were developed in natural gray squirrel, ermine, sable and chinchilla. Many contrasting furs, such as squirrel and ermine, were often combined. Elaborate evening wraps were even trimmed with real

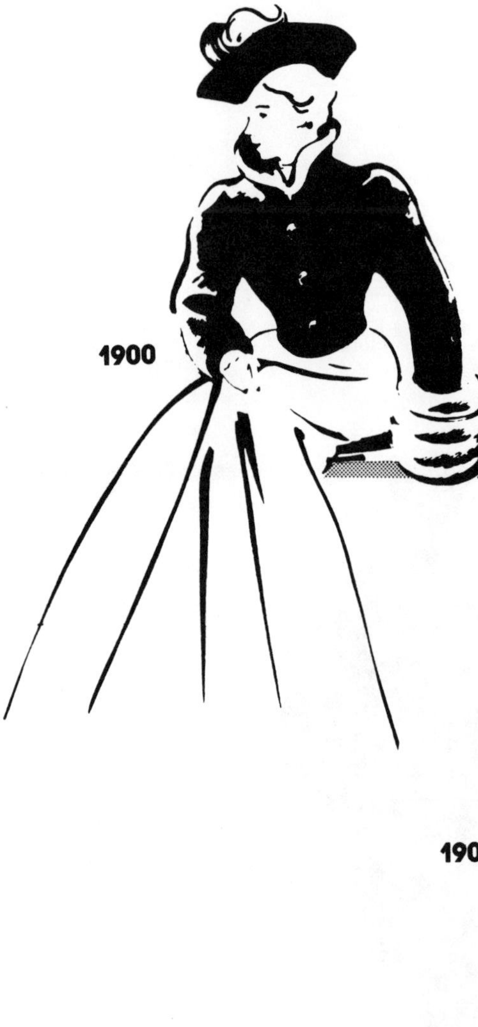

1902

1902

lace, either as a collar coming down below the fur collar or down the front of the coat.

The **1902** double silver fox scarf was the predecessor of the big fashion of the thirties and also the single fox scarf fashion of the twenties. Our squirrel coat, **1902**, is softened with cape and small collar.

By **1912** the large muff had come into its own. We find this worn with the single fox scarf and also with the long stole. We have also illustrated white fox which had a tremendous popularity at this time, along with all varieties of fox and other long-haired furs. The stole in our sketch is made of

skunk, but other furs were used, varying from those with long hair to the shorter-haired types—mink, squirrel and sealskin.

This was also the great period for the long, fitted black ponyskin coat with black lynx collars. The older woman turned to black caracul and for a time there seemed very little variety although some beaver coats were worn. However, beaver had two disadvantages: it was very heavy and the hair curled when exposed to rain or dampness.

Fur coats reflected the lines of the cloth coat in the 1920s. In **1924** we find the sumptuous chinchilla wraparound coat and by **1926** the ermine evening wrap, bulky at

1924

1912

1912

1926

1926

1934

the top. This is also the beginning of the mink coat as we know it today, although mink had been used as far back as sealskin. In **1926** furs for people of modest incomes were made possible by using natural muskrat, often of three-quarter length, with the pelts of the animals seamed without being worked into strips.

By **1934** more subtle tailoring had come in with the fitted broadtail full length styles. The model sketched is by Worth. This same year the collarless fox jacket, which was the delight of women for both daytime and evening wear for such a long time, was also launched. A **1937** model is illustrated.

Nutria was a very popular fur all through the twenties because it was less bulky than beaver. The model illustrated is dated **1938**.

The **1941** Persian lamb coat had a square shoulderline and rippling back fullness. This silhouette dominated fur coats of the early forties. It was also popular in sheared beaver.

Dyeing and shearing of beaver created a velvety, supple fur with a silvery sheen. The **1950** beaver coat had a completely different silhouette: long, loose, hanging almost straight from the shoulder. The shoulderline is natural, not squared. This coat reflected the influence of the New Look.

Dyeing and shearing of fur is one example of improved manufacturing processes. Another essential fur process is "letting out," which became very important when the popularity and availability of mink increased during the fifties.

Before letting out was invented, small skins were sewn together, skin on skin. The result was like patchwork, with all the seams showing. Each seam broke the flow of the silhouette, and coats looked lumpy and bumpy.

When skins are let out, they are sliced into narrow diagonal strips. The strips are sewn together again in a special way on the inside or skin side so that the seams do not show on the outside or fur side. Now the

1941

1937

1938

1950

109

furrier has a long length of fur to work with, instead of many skins. The lengths of fur handle more like fabric. The finished garment is supple, with a flowing silhouette, and relatively few visible seams. Letting out is skilled labor that adds greatly to the cost of the fur garment. Our minks of the fifties are typical of graceful let-out styles.

The jacket, **1951**, a casual style designed to be worn over day or evening dresses. The versatility of mink garments was very much appreciated. Cape stole, **1953**, wraps in front and curves around and down in back. Waist-nipping jacket, **1954**, has dolman sleeves. This jacket could be worn with full or slim skirts. The curving collar was typical of the period, and was often worn turned up around the neck.

Many new mink colors became available as mink farms were established to breed animals. As a new color or "mutation" ap-

1951

1953

1954

1955

peared it was bred and developed to increase the supply. Thus, in addition to brown shades, there were all sorts of beige tones, gray-blue tones and smoky taupe tones. Deep brown approached black, though the true black mink is dyed. Natural white mink must be bleached to hold its color. Mink became so popular during the fifties that furriers worried about a "one-fur" market. It was certainly true that few women wanted persian lamb and fox, furs, which had commanded tremendous prestige in the forties.

The well-to-do woman who owned mink and wanted a second fur sometimes chose Russian broadtail, a lightweight, delicate fur with the appearance of fine silk brocade fabric. Our three-quarter broadtail coat is dated **1955**. It has a sable collar, an expression of the fur-on-fur theme. The **1957** bubble or cocoon coat shows mink

worked horizontally. This was a high-fashion silhouette of its time, suggesting the shapes of Balenciaga. It also recalls pre-1920 fashions. (See 1919, Coats.)

Long-haired furs lost ground with a few exceptions, for instance, the white fox ski parka, **1958**.

There was a revival of chinchilla as a luxury fur during the fifties. Small capes and stoles commanded prestige as evening wraps. For those who could afford the price, there were dramatic full-length coats, often worked horizontally.

This casual use of fur was prophetic, as in the **1959** mink "bathrobe" coat that wrapped and tied casually at the waist with a kind of throwaway chic. The **1960** Somali leopard coat moved away from the body, flaring from a high, lightly marked waistline. Hemlines were rising. (This is essen-

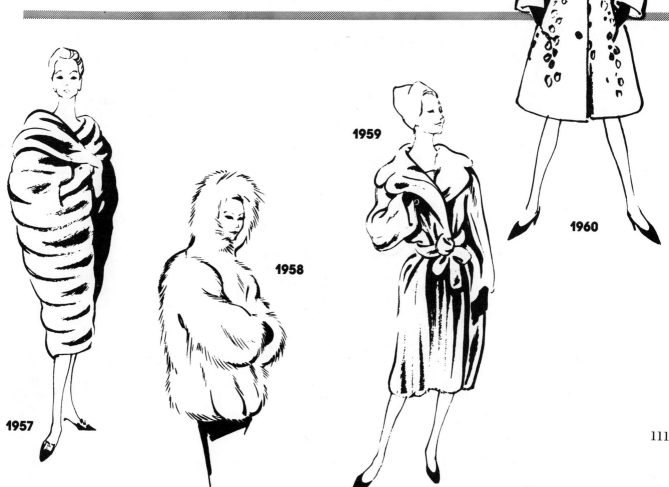

1957

1958

1959

1960

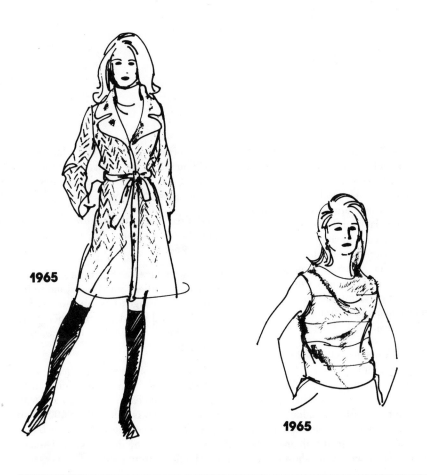

1965

1965

tially a loose coat, but very shapely compared to the 1950 beaver.)

Attitudes toward fur as well as fur fashions were also changing. There was public concern for endangered species of animals.

Eventually, American furriers stopped working with most spotted cats, which were in danger of extinction. However, even at the peak of their popularity, the cats accounted for a very small percentage of total fur garments sold.

Concern for endangered species was one reason why some women did not wear specific furs like the spotted cats. But opposition to all furs came from organized groups whose members opposed the killing of fur-bearing animals as a matter of principle. They endorsed "fake furs" as substitutes. Though furriers worried about the impact of the synthetic fabrics simulating fur, in the long run, fake furs were not successful.

There was still another problem for furriers

as the 1960s began. Young women thought fur was old-fashioned and dowdy. Mature women adored mink coats and stoles, but their daughters did not share that adoration. Furriers realized that there was a need for younger, more casual styles at lower prices.

During the sixties, "old" furs were revived. Pony skin, curly lambs, fox, raccoon and fitch appeared again in coats and jackets.

One of the most important innovations of the sixties, was the "piecing" of furs, mainly mink. Scraps of pelts previously discarded were sewn together to form patterns including tweed, stripe, check, chevron and herringbone effects. Use of leftover scraps and elimination of the expensive letting out process substantially lowered the cost of these coats. Their colorings and youthful styling appealed to many younger women who could not afford to spend thousands of dollars on traditional minks. Eventually other furs were pieced, for example,

1968

1973

1987

fox and sable. The new, young-looking, less expensive fashions were known as "fun furs," an ill-chosen name for these attractive styles. The **1965** coat is in "pastel" pieced mink, a soft brown and white, worked in a chevron effect.

Even traditional mink showed the influence of ready-to-wear styling. Our white mink over-blouse has a fashionable cowl neckline and is worked horizontally. It is dated **1965**. The long, **1968** double-breasted coat is of broadtail lamb dyed beige. It was inspired by the fashions of the film *Dr. Zhivago*, set in nineteenth-century Russia.

Acceptance of pants in 1970 spurred interest in jackets. We show a **1973** waist-length jacket of long-haired raccoon mounted on leather.

During the 1970s, women wore jackets with pants as well as with skirts.

In the 1980s, fur prices came down as manufacturing moved overseas, where production costs were lower. Furs were now reach-ing a wide customer audience. The full length coat in a classic style was a number one favorite, especially in mink; though other furs, like fox and raccoon, were also popular.

Though most women put their money in classics or near-classics, there were designers who handled luxury furs in special ways for those women who could afford them. We show a golden sable jacket by Fendi, **1987**, with fur worked in semi-circular bands to accentuate the cocoon silhouette.

While more women were wearing fur at the end of the 1980s, there was also growing opposition to the wearing of fur. The organized groups that had gathered strength in the 1960s gained much attention and support in the 1980s. Again, clothing designers introduced coats in synthetic fabrics imitating furs. Whether those imitations would be more successful the second time round was an open question at the end of the decade.

10
SILHOUETTES

As the twentieth century begins, inflexible rules of modesty still govern fashion.

1900 Daytime necklines are high. Legs and ankles are unseen. A tightly laced corset thrusts the body forward in an S-shaped curve. Bosom and hips are generously curved in contrast to a small waist. Shoulder width comes from puffed "leg-o'-mutton" sleeves. Skirts are still full, worn over petticoats. This is the hour-glass figure idealized in the drawings of Charles Dana Gibson.

1910 The silhouette narrows as full skirts and the S-shaped body curve disappear. The waist is still pinched and corseted. The hobble skirt tapers towards the hem and is so restrictive that women must walk with little, mincing steps—a good example of how fashion affects movement and gesture. The hobble skirt didn't last long, but skirts stayed relatively narrow and began to rise, so that ankles could sometimes be seen.

1919 The tubular silhouette is softer and more natural. The dress is belted but the waist is not pinched; it's just not important.

1900

1910

1919

1926

116

The hemline is almost at mid-calf. Draping, tiers and tunics created fullness at the hipline; these are treatments of the dress itself, in contrast to the pads and bustles of the nineteenth century. Hemlines are moving up and down and will go down again. But legs and feet are now seen, and hosiery and shoes are important. In this silhouette, the hair is upswept and arranged in a classic Grecian knot, an alternative to the new, daring short cuts.

1926 The boyish, straight-up-and-down silhouette ignores bustline, waist and hips. Some women bind their breasts to flatten them. While there are still corsets, many women go without. Skirts stop at the knee, a new high. Though the waist is not marked, there are some indications of a low waistline. One such indication is the coat that buttons low, at the hip, as in this silhouette. The cloche hat pulls down over very short, cropped hair.

1931 Skirt hemlines drop suddenly in 1930 and the silhouette changes. Now bustline, waist and hip are marked, but not accentuated. Clothes are softer, as in this silhouette, with its flared skirt. Hair is longer and waved. The cropped, boyish cuts of the 1920s are out.

1938 Hemlines have been rising steadily during the 1930s. Now the shoulderline is moving out; puffed sleeves are often an expression of shoulder width. (Compare with silhouette of 1900.) The waistline is more definitely marked now. Women still wear corsets or girdles, as they are called. The peasant blouse or sweater worn with a dirndl skirt is an expression of interest in folkloric fashion. Hair is longer and wavy; or straight and curled or turned under at the ends.

1944 The shoulderline is now wide and padded. Bust and waist are marked, hips are slim, skirts are only moderately full, because of wartime restrictions on use of fabric. The big-brimmed cartwheel hat balances the silhouette. Shoes have round toes.

1944

1938

1931

117

1947 Christian Dior launches his "New Look." Shoulder pads and the military influences of the wartime years disappear. The silhouette is almost Victorian, with uplifted bustline, the first pinched waist since the early 1900s and a rounded hipline. Women wear uplift bras, waist cinchers and full, stiff petticoats. Hemlines are eight to ten inches off the ground. Shoes change, too; toes are pointed and heels are narrow. Hair is short, curly and close to the head. Almost immediately, as in 1930, skirt hemlines begin to rise, but the essentials of the New Look continue through the 1950s.

1958 A Chanel suit reflects the trend away from restrictive New Look fashions. The shoulderline is natural, with a high armhole. The semi-fitted jacket foreshadows the return of the chemise. The jacket, and the easy skirt, reaching to just below the knee, are typical of Chanel. Shoes still have stiletto heels and pointed toes.

1965 The chemise evolves from the work of designers like Balenciaga, known for his architectural shapes. Shoulders are natural, the waist is unmarked, hemlines are ending above the knee. Shoes have low or flat heels and sharply pointed toes are gone. Textured and colored pantyhose and tights coordinate with clothing and with shoes.

1969 Variations of the chemise are still the dominant silhouette. The shortest length is shorter than ever before—a dress that barely covers the thighs. The silhouette shows a chemise that flares from the shoulderline to a moderately full hem. The corsets and girdles of earlier times are becoming obsolete; women wear fewer undergarments than ever before. Tights or pantyhose, though, are essential. Legs are on display as never before. (Compare 1969 to the silhouette of the 1920s.)

1970 Women wear pants on the street. This is in reaction to the introduction of the

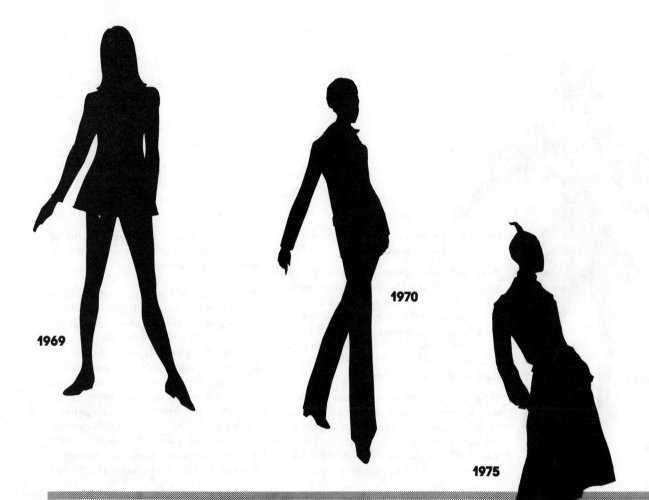

1969

1970

1975

1978

midi, a mid-calf length skirt. Though the fashion establishment endorses the midi, women reject it; the change is too sudden. The tailored jacket covers the hips. Trousers are slightly flared. These pants are worn with low-heeled demi-boots or oxfords; later, women will wear pants with high heels.

1975 The silhouette is soft and natural. Skirts have been coming down gradually and the hemline is now just below the knee. Waist and hipline are marked, but not exaggerated. Shoulderline is natural. Women are turning, more and more, to separates for all daytime occasions—and some dress-up occasions. The bloused jacket or sweater and the flared skirt are typical separates of the mid-1970s. Shoes have round toes.

1978 Skirt hemlines move up a few inches, then down a few inches in the late 1970s, but the trend is towards longer lengths. Blousing, fullness, ease and a casual atti-

119

1981

tude, even in dressy clothes, is characteristic of the end of the decade.

1981 Silhouette from Norma Kamali's flippy dress. The wider shoulderline, moving into full sleeves and a gathered bodice, is an example of the "big shirt" that developed from the oversized Annie Hall look. The smooth, sleek hip is in contrast to fullness above and below. The brief skirt foreshadows the return of the mini.

1987 A new designer, Christian Lacroix, sets the fashion world on its ear with his "pouf" silhouette. It combines a closely fitted bodice with a short, full, round skirt that recalls the skirts of the eighteenth and nineteenth centuries. The pouf does not

last long, because it's impractical. But it makes so much noise and news that it is of historical importance.

1989 The idea of long over short has been developing since the mid-1980s. This 1989 version poses a sweater over tights. It recalls the 1969 mini, though the lines are different. Shoulder pads are on the way out again and shoulderlines are more rounded. Again, bustline and waistline are not marked; there is a contrast between the bulk of the top and the leggings. Short boots with low heels and round toes finish off the silhouette. Comparing this to the 1969 chemise silhouette raises an interesting question: Will the skirt disappear entirely?

1987

1989

11

A C C E S S O R I E S

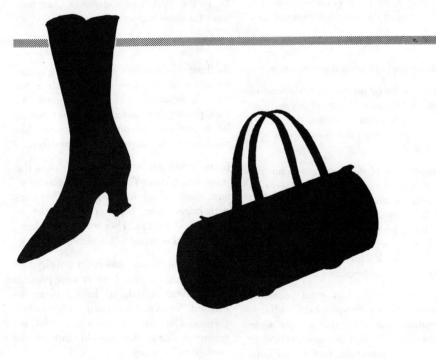

Accessories take their cues from clothing; they change as the width of the shoulderline and the level of the hemline change; they

began to lose their power during World War II, in the 1940s; so did gloves, but hats were far more important.

accentuate and enhance the silhouette.

Accessories can be functional or decorative or both. A woman's choice of accessories can create her unique fashion image; her ability to "play" with accessories can be a mark of real chic.

The importance of each category changes from decade to decade, or even year to year. Some accessories have disappeared completely, or almost completely, while others have become essential. Fans and parasols disappeared in the 1920s, while handbags gained. Hosiery became an accessory when skirt hemlines rose.

The 1930s were the last great years for neckwear—those crisp white collars, cuffs, jabots and gilets that women wore with tailored suits and dresses. Neckwear had to look immaculate; that meant constant laundering. Women no longer wanted to spend time on such chores.

Hats, the all-time, great-great accessory,

By the end of the 1950s, there was a vogue for status accessories marked with a designer's signature, initial or trademark. As time passed, licensing of designer names for accessories became highly profitable when the name carried enough prestige.

In the 1960s accessories helped define the youth revolution. Young women wore platform shoes, clogs and sneakers. They carried huge, limp bags or knapsacks of leather and canvas. They wore cotton bandannas and scorned silk scarves.

African and Native American jewelry, art nouveau and art deco jewelry were popular in the 1960s and later. Ethnic ideas included Native American and cowboy themes. The term, "retro" was coined, referring to things that are old, but not old enough to be antique.

We show a sampling of accessories of the century; readers with long fashion memories may add their own favorites.

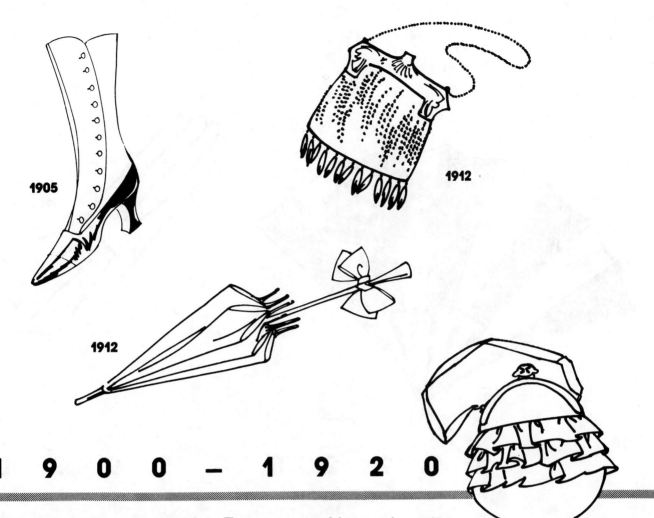

1905

1912

1912

1916

1 9 0 0 — 1 9 2 0

Hats were the dominant accessory of the early 1900s. Shoes and hosiery were hidden under long skirts. Handbags were small and ladylike. The parasol was often matched to a specific dress or costume.

Buttoned boot, **1905**, for "motoring," a new pastime for ladies. Combinations of fabric and leather were popular. The button was a "modern" improvement on lacing.

Silvery metallic mesh bag, **1912**, set on a metal frame, dangling from a silvery chain, with metal fringe. A style with a long fashion life.

Parasol, **1912**, finished off with a bow.

There were more elaborate styles, with lace, shirring and ruffling. Parasols were also known as "sunshades," for they were designed to protect complexions from the sun. Suntanned skin was considered vulgar.

Ruffled "hoopskirt" bag of heavy black "armure" silk, **1916**. It was set on a metal frame, and anticipated the modern pouch.

Two-button shoe, **1917**, combined black leather and satin, with jet embroidery. Hemlines were on the rise. Shoes were becoming more important. This shoe seemed to bridge the gap between boot and pump.

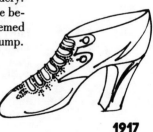

1917

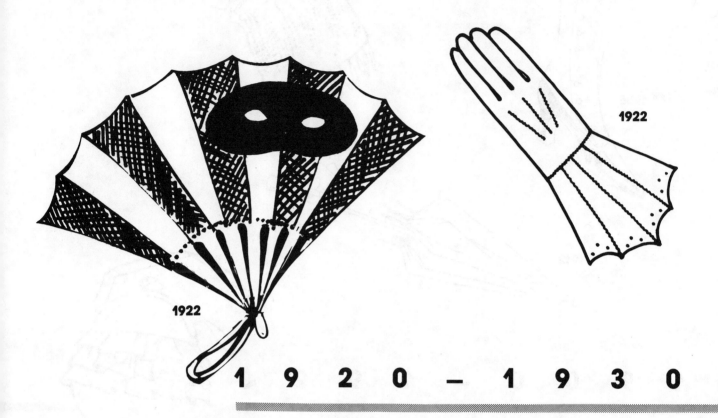

1922

1922

1 9 2 0 — 1 9 3 0

The angular lines of art deco influenced accessories of the twenties. Small accessories such as compacts and cigarette cases were among the most beautiful examples of art deco of the period.

Fan, **1922**, of silk panels with appliquéd velvet mask to peep through—perfect accessory for a "vamp."

Gauntlet glove of gray leather embroidered with red to accent pointed art deco lines, **1922**.

Strapped pump, **1922**, a sport shoe with a fairly low, chunky heel. (Compare with hollow French heel of 1905 shoe.) In "fawn" (soft brown) suede with blue leather trim. Perforated detailing suggests spectator pump to come.

Oxford tie, **1926**, a new version of the old-fashioned laced boot. Gray suede with red patent leather trim.

Brocade pump, **1926**, with "colonial" tongue, oval enamel ornament at instep; a dressy shoe.

Softly gathered black suede bag on metal frame, **1927**, loose side flap concealing a mirror, useful for women who want to refresh their makeup.

Bracelet, gold and silver, **1927**, an example of the new "tailored" jewelry. The rectangular shape is known as "baguette," from the French word for long loaves of bread.

Pouch bag, **1928**, embroidered, quilted, flame-colored silk, on amber-colored frame.

1922

1926

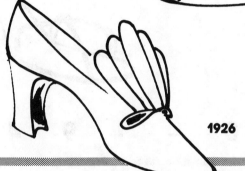

1926

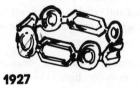

1927

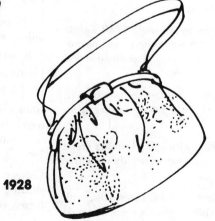

1928

1927

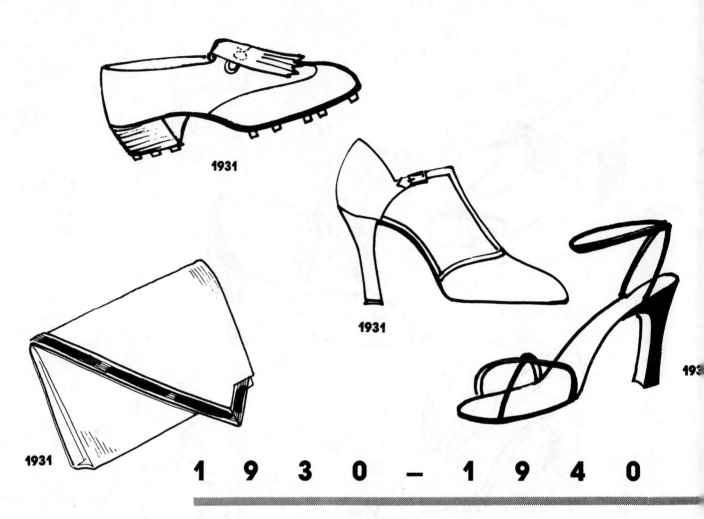

1931

1931

1931

193

1 9 3 0 — 1 9 4 0

1936

The large, slim envelope bag held under the arm was typical of the 1930s. Narrow leather belts and wider, crushed styles marked the waistline. Flower jewelry of glass and metal was popular; fabric flowers were pinned on suit lapels or tucked into the hair. Low-heeled shoes were still only for active sportswear.

Gilet and cuffs by Chanel, **1930**, white linen, edged with white piqué and narrow black velvet ribbon; a subtle contrast of textures as well as color.

Art deco-influenced envelope bag in smooth leather with patent leather trim, **1931**.

Golf shoe, **1931**, with spiked rubber crepe sole; a no-nonsense style strictly for active sportswear.

"Barefoot" sandal, **1931**, black silk, with ankle strap. Though this shoe was designed for evening wear, it was shown in a magazine of the day with copy noting that ". . . the barefoot sandal has even been seen by day—at garden parties and cocktails."

"Resort" T-strap sandal, **1931**, white suede. After the game, for lunch in the country club.

Belt of crushed red patent leather, **1931**. Draping and crushing of leather as if it were fabric was in keeping with softened silhouettes.

Suede pump, **1933**, with "dressmaker" detailing on vamp; high sides and throat.

Belt, **1935**, navy leather with red and navy plastic art deco buckle in shape described as "Egyptian temple."

Gardenia clip earrings, **1936**, of enameled metal. Some clips could be worn as earrings or as pins. Or, they were worn in matched "sets."

Crescent pouch bag by Molyneux, with soft shirring, **1936**. One example of the new larger, softer shapes in brown calf.

Square bag by Schiaparelli, **1936**, brown calf. Another soft shape with plenty of inside room. The bracelet handle slipped over the wrist.

126

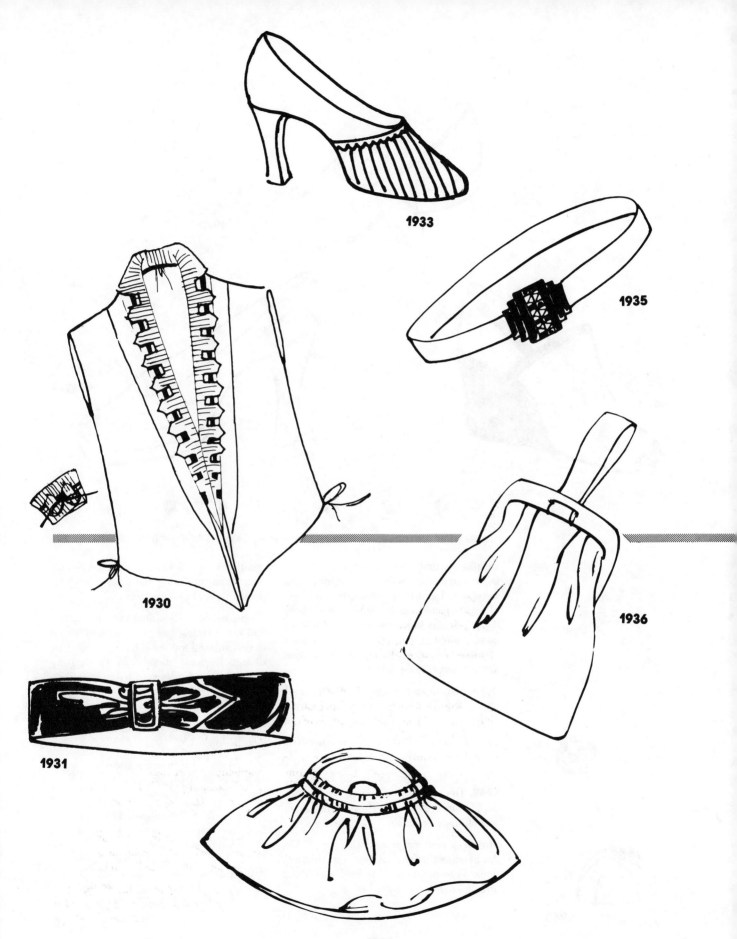

1933

1935

1930

1936

1931

1936

127

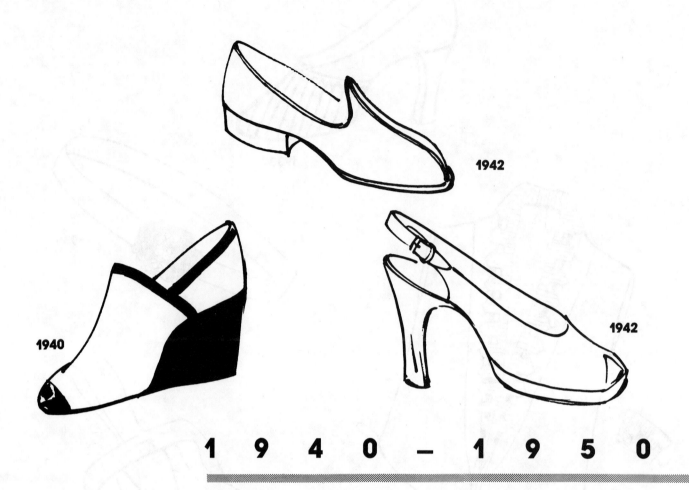

1942

1940

1942

1 9 4 0 – 1 9 5 0

Despite wartime restrictions on the use of fabric and leather, accessories of the forties were varied and imaginative. If two kinds of leather could not be used in one shoe, then designers turned to fabric and leather combinations. The wedge and platform soles that began at the end of the thirties carried over into the forties.

Open-toed wedgie pump, **1940**, red and navy suede; a daytime shoe. This was a high wedge.

Leopard hatpin, **1940**, a last touch of frivolity before wartime austerity.

"Shank's Mare" by Evins for I. Miller, **1942**. The first flat-heeled shoe widely accepted for street wear. This early version was of black buckskin.

Slingback platform pump, open toe, **1942**. An average platform. A few were higher. Some were narrower. The heel was high, and tapered downwards.

Small box bag, **1943**, black plastic patent, with a mirror lining the lid. A popular dressy style of the war years.

Suede over-the-shoulder bag, by Koret, **1943**, the largest bag yet. It closed with a drawstring and was not set on a frame. This design became classic. With it, long "crushed" suede gloves with flaring cuffs—descended from the gauntlets of the 1920s.

Large clutch bag of rayon fabric with linen texture, **1944**. Wooden frame replaced metal.

Shirred rayon matte jersey glove, a glamour accessory of **1944**, for dress wear. Fabric substituted for leather.

Pastel suede ballet slipper, **1946**, evolved from professional Capezio ballet slipper first worn by young women on the street in 1944. An early youth fad. Soft leather and drawstring tie were a new look for shoes.

1940

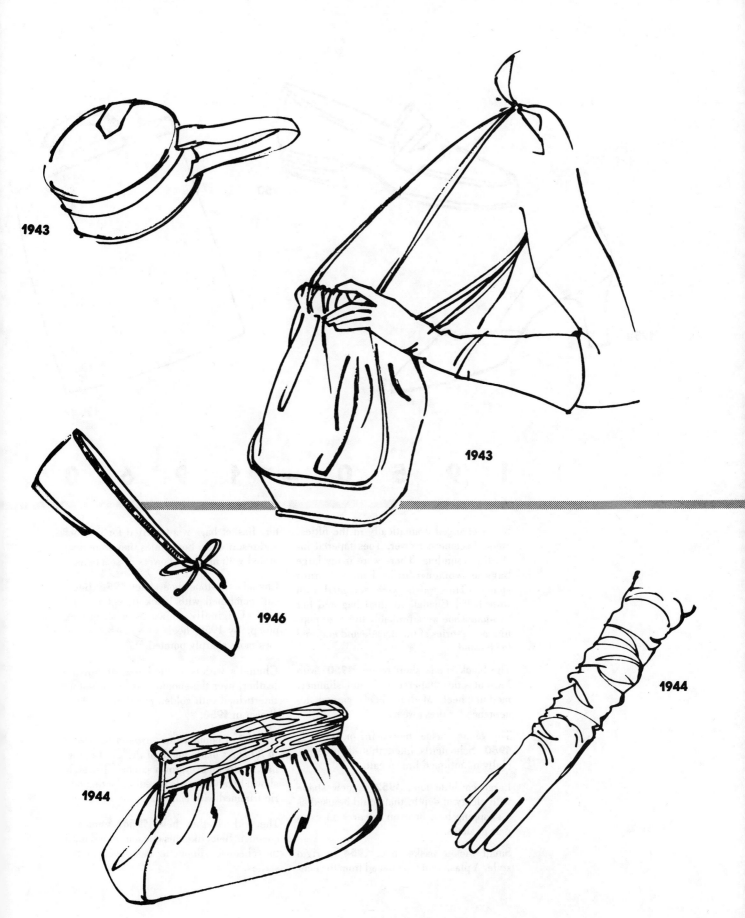

1943

1943

1946

1944

1944

1944

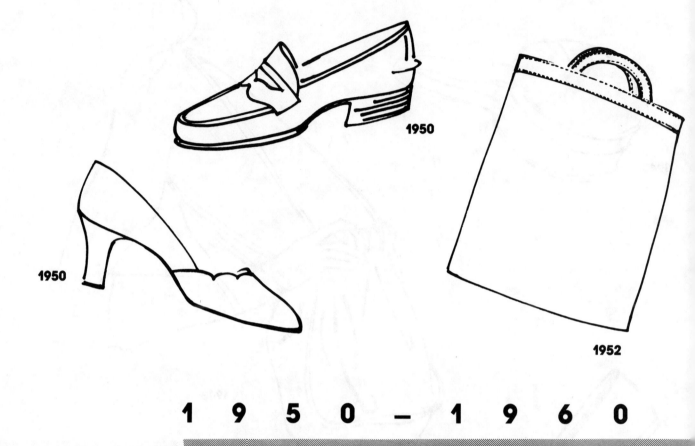

1950

1950

1952

1 9 5 0 – 1 9 6 0

Shoes changed dramatically in the fifties. Heels became narrower. Toes tapered instead of rounding. There were many large bags as women required more "inner space." Tiny waists were accented with wide belts. Chanel's quilted bag and her two-tone shoe were probably the most popular accessories of the decade and endured far beyond.

The black suede shell pump, **1950**, with low-cut sides, tapered toe, and slimmer, medium heel. Medium heels gained acceptance for dress wear.

The young, casual moccasin, or "loafer," **1950**. Schoolgirls liked this shoe, especially in antiqued brown calf.

Large cowhide tote, **1952**, a new shape with plenty of depth, that could be used as a shopping bag, or even to carry an extra pair of shoes.

Small wicker basket bag, **1954**, a rigid style. A plastic lid top opened from the cen-

ter. Basket bags were carried for summer and resort wear. Sometimes they were decorated with artificial flowers or seashells.

Chanel's two-tone shoe, dated **1956**. Beige calf combined with black patent tip and heel. Originally shown as a slingback pump. By 1956, heels were narrower and toes more sharply pointed.

Chanel's widely copied bag of quilted leather; over-the-shoulder strap of leather intertwined with golden metal chain. First shown in **1956**.

In **1957**, a popular film, *Around the World in 80 Days* made much of the giant carpet bag, really an overgrown satchel. The style shown here was made of real carpeting fabric trimmed with leather.

The wide leather belt, **1958**, almost a corselet. Belts like this one continued until the chemise silhouette took over in the sixties.

130

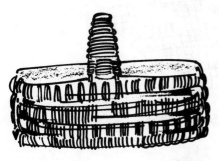

1954

1956

1956

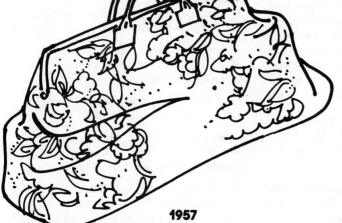

1957

1958

131

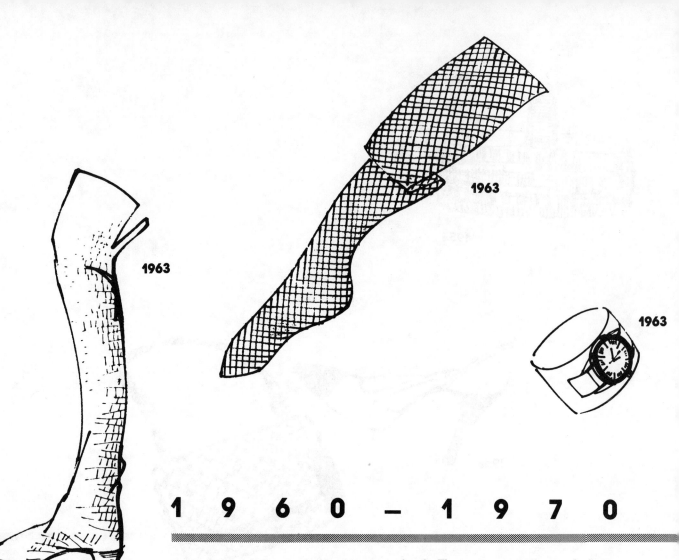

1963

1963

1963

1963

1 9 6 0 — 1 9 7 0

Boots, textured hosiery and tights became important accessories during the sixties as the silhouette changed again. Never had so much leg showed. Pointy-toe shoes gradually rounded, and heels lowered until they were pancake-flat. Tiny bags were so insufficient that women began to carry two bags: a small one plus a large tote. Watches became high fashion. Women—and men—collected Native American and African jewelry.

White kid boot, flat heel, launched by Courrèges; the signature accessory of the decade, from **1963** on.

Deluxe over-the-knee alligator boot, **1963**, Saint Laurent, a prestige fashion, high-priced, limited, but significant.

Fishnet stocking, **1963**, one of many textures. Later, waist-high tights replaced hosiery as hemlines rose.

Sport watch, **1963**, set on wide leather band. There was a trend towards larger watches with more colorful straps.

Gladiator sandal, **1964**, one of many styles that wrapped high, in the manner of Greek and Roman sandals.

Driving glove, **1966**, one-button fastening at wrist. Shown with cotton palm and perforated leather back.

Mary Jane pump, **1967**, flat heel, rounded toe, part of the little girl look.

"Treasure chest" bag, **1968**, leather with metallic lock and trim. A rigid satchel with handle, recalling box bags of the forties.

Soft leather luggage bag, **1968**, large and double-handled. Named for its zippers, compartments and pockets, which suggested a suitcase. Often used for traveling.

Turquoise and silver pins and "squash blossom" necklace, all traditional Navajo designs, **1969**. Native American jewelry became fashionable in the late 1960s.

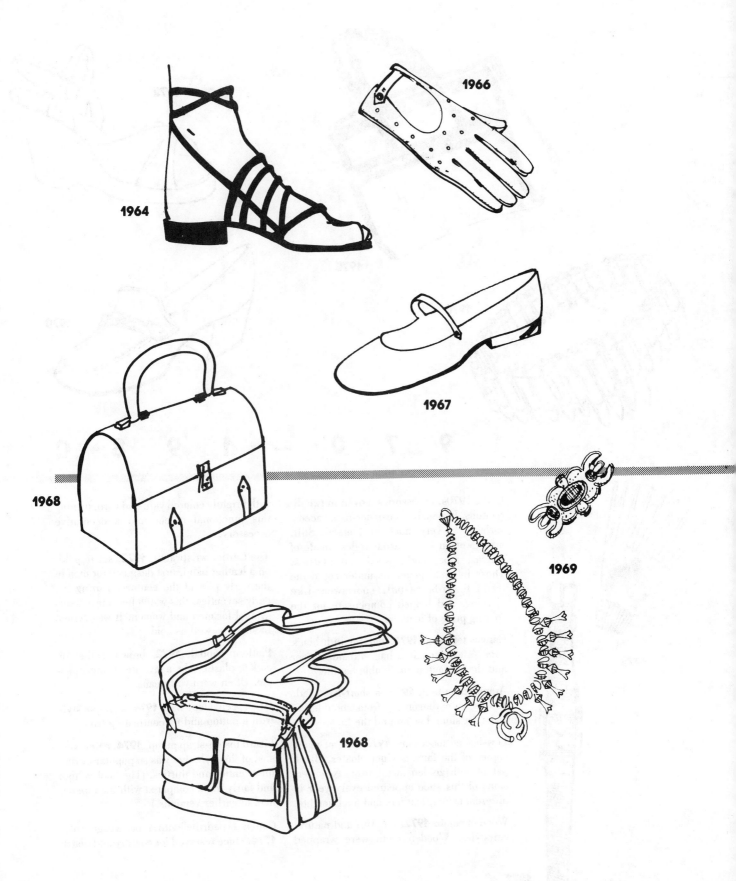

1964

1966

1967

1968

1968

1969

133

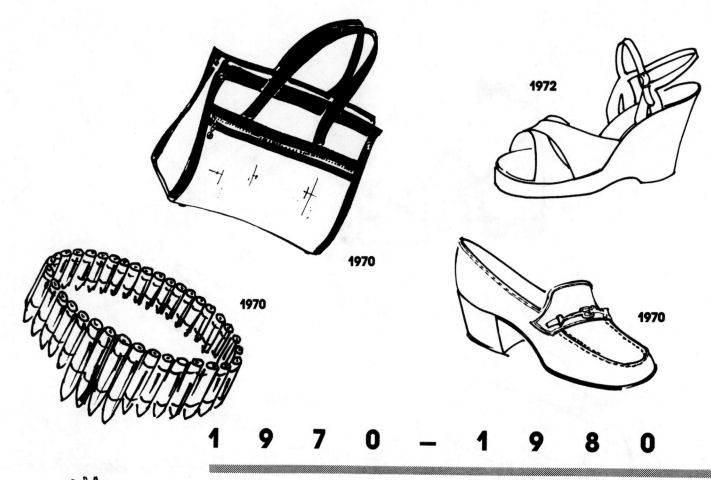

1972

1970

1970

1970

1970

1972

1972

1 9 7 0 — 1 9 8 0

In the 1970s, accessories moved in two directions. Expensive, designer-name accessories were very much in demand. Still, many women wore casual styles, made of canvas, rope, cork, wood and plastics. Those informal materials underscored the trend towards casual, sportswear-like clothing, and helped compensate for the soaring price of leathers.

Canvas tote bag, **1970**, natural with black trim. A large spacious bag with side zipper and the characteristic double handle.

Ammunition belt, **1970**, a short-lived fad. It was worn diagonally from shoulder to waist, or slung low around the hips.

Low-heeled moccasin, **1970**, one of many copies of the famous Gucci loafer. Black patent with golden metal trim. New versions of this shoe appeared every year in different colors, leathers and heel heights.

Wooden comb, **1972**, for Afro and natural hairstyles. Wooden teeth were wrapped

with brightly colored yarn and wire, turning this functional object into a decorative accessory.

The Cartier wristwatch, **1972**, set in gold, on a leather band, first designed for men in the early part of the century. During the early seventies, this watch became a status symbol for men and women. It was copied in silver as well as gold.

Platform sandal, **1972**, brown leather on cork or plastic sole, a favorite of young people. Often worn with jeans.

Hermes envelope bag, **1974**, a simple style with a button and no contrasting trim.

Lizard instep-strap pump, **1974**, a new version of the style that was so popular during the twenties and thirties. (The heel is high and fairly thick compared with the tapered heel of earlier versions.)

Cotton espadrille with rope wedge sole, **1974**. Once reserved for country and beach

1974

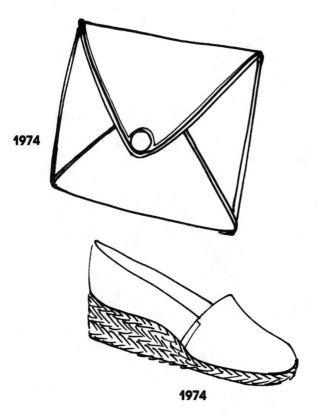

1974

1974

1975

1976

wear, the espadrille took to city streets in
1974.

Louis Vuitton duffle bag, of brown vinyl-
coated canvas stamped with "LV" ini-
tials—the same material this maker used
for its luggage. **1975**.

The free-form sterling silver belt buckle on
a leather belt, by Elsa Peretti, was typical
of her clean-cut, innovative shapes. This
version can be dated **1976**, but remained
popular through the 1980s.

Wooden bangle bracelet set with glass
"stones," by Bonwillum, **1978**.

Minaudiere (evening bag) by Rafael San-
chez, **1978**, made of polished, grained
wood, finished with a silk tassel.

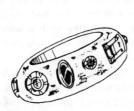

1978

1978

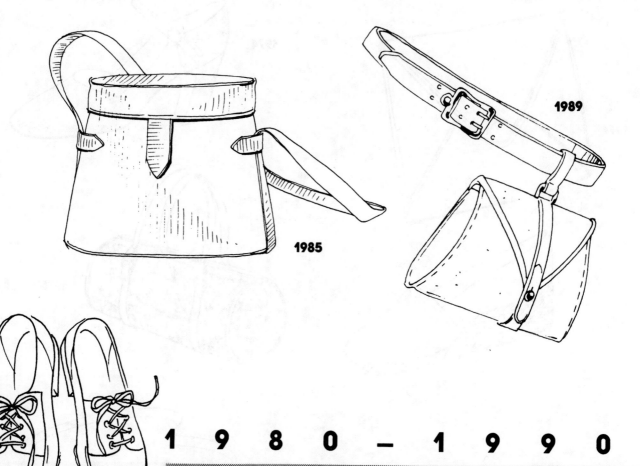

1985

1989

1980

1 9 8 0 — 1 9 9 0

In the 1980s, the range of accessories was so wide, that themes sometimes seemed to contradict each other. Inexpensive, colorful, amusing watches were fashionable—and so were expensive status watches. Smart flat and low-heeled shoes and athletic shoes were standard footwear—and so was the high-heeled pump. Sunglasses grew larger, until smaller styles came into fashion. Clothes were simpler and less constructed every year, and accessories were more important than ever.

"Jellies" were named for their material: glossy, molded rubber, in deep and bright colors. These oxfords, by Andrew Geller, **1980**.

Handbag shaped like camera bag, of ribbed leather, by Bagheera, **1985**, typical of more rigid styles based on functional shapes.

Belt bag, to free hands and keep money secure, in canvas with leather, **1989**, by Isaac Mizrahi for Corinne Rogers.

Jagged edge suede pump, Andrea Pfister, **1985**.

"Headlight" necklace of large crystals set in bezels (rims), Kenneth Jay Lane, **1985**.

Large sunglasses with black and tortoise rims, Laura Biagiotti for Private Eyes, **1987**.

Sunglasses in squared-off, narrow shape, Alain Mikli, **1988**.

Star earrings, gold metal, in shoulder-sweeping length, Patrick Kelly, **1989**.

Summer version of Swatch Watch®, in pastels, with novel dial, plastic band, quartz movement, **1989**.

Big drawstring bag, **1989**, combines smooth and crocodile-embossed leather.

Ghillie lacing, boot shoe in suede, Diego Della Valle, **1989**.

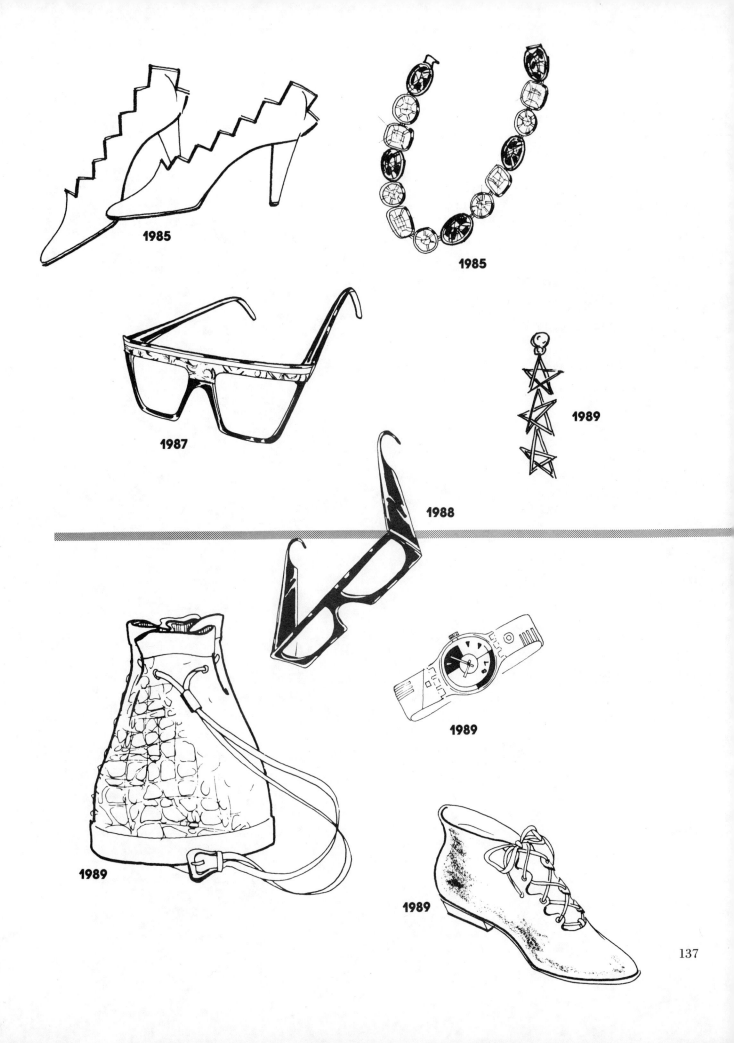

1985

1985

1987

1989

1988

1989

1989

1989

137

I N D E X